Sustainability Jobs
The Complete Guide to Landing Your Dream Green Job

By Kevin Wilhelm
Annie Thomas   Katie Thompson   Ruth Lee

Printed in the United States of America

First Printing, 2016

ISBN 978-1-365-38612-1

Sustainable Business Consulting
4700 42nd Ave SW, Suite 535
Seattle, WA 98116

www.sustainabilitygreenjobs.com

ABOUT THE AUTHOR

Kevin Wilhelm is the CEO of Sustainable Business Consulting and is one of the world's pre-eminent business consultants and teachers in the field of sustainability. He has conducted over 600 career sessions with individuals ranging from college students to career professionals in their 40's and 50's.

He has over 21 years of experience working with 115+ businesses ranging across 37 different industries - from Fortune 500 multinationals to small businesses, from government agencies to non-profits. His firm specializes in helping organizations realize business value through the integration of sustainability into everything they do.

Some of his firm's clients include Nordstrom, REI, Alaska Airlines, The North Face, Expeditors, Redbox, Drugstore.com, American Seafoods, Roy Farms and Real Networks to name a few.

He is the author of two acclaimed books in this field:
- *Return on Sustainability: How Business Can Increase Profitability & Address Climate Change in an Uncertain Economy*
- *Making Sustainability Stick: The Blueprint for Successful Sustainability Implementation*

He has also been a contributing writer on five other publications including:

- *Advancing Sustainability in Higher Education* (2007)
- *Green Jobs: a Guide to Eco-Friendly Employment* (2008)
- *Go Green Rating Scale for Early Childhood Settings* (2010)
- *Intro to Sustainable Business (2015) Video textbook available on Safari Books only*
- *The Reducetarian Solution (2017)*

He has taught 12 different business courses on sustainability at seven institutions and has given over 300 lectures across the country.

ACKNOWLEDGEMENTS

I want to thank all of my friends and colleagues who encouraged me to write this book. I especially want to thank my good friend and business partner Ruth Lee, who has been so instrumental in helping me develop this content from day one, and my two colleagues Annie Thomas and Katie Thompson for all their hard work in pulling this together into one book.

I want to thank my wife, Jo. She has been my inspiration throughout this entire career path. She is the one who turned me onto environmentalism. She has been my rock and supported me emotionally after the first 64 conversations that I had with people to start my career in sustainability went nowhere, and she amazes me in her ability to get up each and every day before the crack of dawn, bike to work over eight miles each way, then workout and hit her desk and put in nine to ten hours each day before biking home. There truly is nobody on earth like you JO. You are my inspiration, my backbone, and my reason for being.

I also want to thank the following friends who all deserve thanks not just from me, but from the readers. These individuals provided their input for this book during very busy times personally and professionally and did so in a very short period of time.

Masters that generously provided their time and thoughts for this book:

Name	Position	Organization
Michael Sadowski	Director, Innovation Scale & Partnerships	Nike
Kevin Hagen	CSR Director	Iron Mountain
Jake Swenson	Director of Sustainability	Staples
Molly Ray	Sr. Mgr Sustainability	Office Depot
Janice Lichtenwaldt	Sr. Mgr IT Communications	T-Mobile
Brenna Davis	Director of Sustainability	Virginia Mason
Howard Sharfstein	Associate General Counsel – Environmental Sustainability	Kimberly Clark
Jacqueline Drumheller	Sustainability Manager	Alaska Airlines
Cynthia Figge	Co-Founder and COO	CSR Hub
Ben Packard	Director of Corporate Engagements	The Nature Conservancy
Matt O'Laughlin	Sustainability Manager	K2 Sports
Marsha Willard	CEO	Axis Performance Advisors
Sarah Martinez	Sustainability Maven	Eco Products
Patrick Drum	Portfolio Manager & Research Analyst	Saturna Capital
Sean Schmidt	Office of Sustainability: Assistant Director of Communications & Programs	University of Washington
Jeremy King	Campus Sustainability Coordinator	Denison University
Marianella Franklin	Chief Sustainability Officer	University of Texas-Rio Grande Valley
Jennifer Opdyke Wilhelm	Senior Ecologist	King County Water & Land Resources
Claudia Capitini	Founder and Principal	Maven Consulting, LLC
Dan Moore	CEO	Pandion Consulting and Facilitation
Dan Stonington	Executive Director	NW Natural Resource Group
Derek Eisel	Director of Sales	Scope 5
Eli Reich	Chief Alchemist	Alchemy Goods
Jon Kroman	CEO	Kroman Law
Katie Mattis Sarver	CEO	Katie Mattis Consulting
Maggie Schilling	Administrative Director	Northern Rockies Conservation Cooperative

TABLE OF CONTENTS

INTRODUCTION

There are three reasons for why I decided to write this book.

1. The first is probably the most personal, because if you are reading this, I was just like you. In 2001, I had just finished my MBA and knew I wanted to get into the field of sustainability, but had no idea how to break into the field.

In fact, the term 'sustainability' or 'sustainable business' wasn't even being used yet. Many people were attaching 'green' to just about anything - green jobs, green economy, green business, etc., but there weren't specific job titles around sustainability or CSR like there are today. All I knew at the time was that I had a set of skills, business acumen and a passion to not only improve the community in which I lived but to protect the environment that I so loved.

When people asked me, "Exactly what do you want to do?" I didn't have an answer; all I knew was that I wanted to help business do better - financially, socially and environmentally. So I talked to as many people as I could. I did informational interviews, I volunteered with multiple organizations, but still, finding the job proved to be elusive. I remember those times all too well and want to provide you with a book that can accelerate your job search.

2. Fast forward to where we are today, where I've done over 600 career sessions (coffees, one-on-ones, webinars and in-person workshops) on 'how to get a job' (in sustainability or business) and I figured that it was time to take what I've been telling people in bits and pieces, write it down and put it all in one place.

3. Lastly, as I've seen many of my colleagues make career changes, whether by choice or because they were let go due to the economy, it seemed like no matter what industry or position (sustainability related or not), the job-seeking fundamentals were the same and many of these colleagues were making the same mistakes.

For example, in my experience, only three out of ten jobs are posted online, yet the very first thing my friends or colleagues would do was to go online and make the following three mistakes:

A. Only look online for jobs and get bummed out when they don't find very many job openings that interest them
B. Apply to the first few jobs that they were remotely qualified for but didn't take the time to tailor their resume or create their elevator pitch for that specific role
C. Send out a blast email to all of their friends with a resume attached with the content similar to this: "I'm looking to make a career change" or "I just got laid off and I'm looking for a new job, if anyone knows of anything, please let me know." Which was even lazier than just looking online because they were basically leaving things up to their friends to find them a job

The results were predictable: nobody landed anything doing it this way.

Therefore I've written this book as a tool for wherever you are in the process - whether you are a student about to graduate, someone looking to make a career change or someone looking to move up in your organization. It has been created to not only provide helpful information, but interactive worksheets as well to help you navigate the process. Good luck. We need you. Our society and our planet are counting on you!

HOW TO USE THIS BOOK

Each person is unique, and each job search is different depending on the point in your life and career each time you begin the process. Therefore, this book is organized around the four key themes listed below with critical learnings, tips from the masters, and worksheets in each section to make the job search process more digestible.

The four main themes for this book:

1. **Getting Clear on What You Want**
   This section is possibly the hardest part and takes the most internal reflection. You'll inventory your skill set, get clear on your elevator pitch and truly decide what you want out of this next job - whether it's experience, more pay, life-work balance or whatever it may be. You will also explore and be inspired by indirect opportunities and paths that can get you where you want to be.

2. **Targeting Your Search and Tailoring Your Resume**
   Narrowing down your job search and tailoring both your pitch and resume is critical to getting the job you want. I'll walk you through how to better target your search and helps you create a list of organizations that you want to go after, as well as how to format and tailor your resume to make your reader say, "Yes!"

3. **Execution**
   How do you get the job? It's all about execution. In the first two sections, we've developed the plan and now it's time to roll up your sleeves and take concrete steps towards your dream job. Since close to 70% of jobs are still found through networking (both traditional and online), I'll focus on building your network and personal brand, developing your plan and then executing during the interview.

4. **Tips from the Masters**
   Learn from 26 leading professionals who have been down the path before you. These top Sustainability Masters share their thoughts, best practices and advice for how to get a job in this field.

ANSWERS TO THE MOST COMMON QUESTIONS

Having done as many career sessions as I've done over the years, common questions arise. Therefore, before you dive into the meat of the book, I've listed the 14 most common questions that I receive and then highlight where in the book you can read more about these.

1. *Where do I get started? What's my first step?*
   This is the most common question I get. It actually doesn't matter. Job searching isn't a linear process. The most important thing is that you mentally decide that you are going to do it, commit to it and just get started. Section 1

2. *What if I have no experience?*
   Then you have to get some. See the section on internships and volunteering. But if you are in an existing job, join the green team or create one at your organization. People no longer hire for these positions based upon the school you attended and GPA - you have to have experience, so get out there and pick some up. Section 2

3. *How did you get your job? Are there any shortcuts?*
   That doesn't matter. What matters is how *you* are going to get *your* job. And unfortunately, there are no shortcuts. Jobs in sustainability are limited. For every posting we put out (even for an internship) we typically receive over 100 resumes within a week. It is a very competitive field - not to mention that finding any job at all is just plain hard work. In my experience, only three in ten jobs are posted online, so networking will be crucial. Section 5

4. *What groups should I join?*
   See the networking section of this book. Section 5

5. *Should I get an internship first?*
   The short answer is that if you are under the age of 25 - yes! This is a very easy way to get your foot in the door. Many companies, including mine, end up hiring their interns if they prove themselves. This is a great way to build your resume, network and gain experience. Section 2

6. *What if I don't see any jobs in Sustainability?*
    Sometimes this is true. You may have to find a way to get creative and create your own job. I had to, and I know many colleagues who had to do the same. They were in another role, and they mentioned that they had an interest in sustainability and somehow responsibility got put onto their shoulders. Then they continued to deliver or run the green team until their superiors realized there was enough work or need to hire them into a sustainability position full-time. Section 2

7. *Where should I look online?*
    Start by looking at the list of websites under the 'where do I look for jobs in this field' section towards the end of this book. Then Google the type of job you are looking for and look at more of the localized sources in your city. Section 5

8. *What books should I read?*
    There is a list of books under 'Books to Read' towards the end of this book. It is an incomplete list, but all of them are valuable. Some of them were the corner stone books of the sustainability movement when it was getting started, while others are more recent, tactical and practical. Section 5

9. *Should I volunteer to gain experience?*
    This all depends on the type of job you are looking for. If where you will be volunteering is directly in alignment or will provide key skills on your resume with the job you want - then yes. You can gain valuable experience and connections anywhere, so volunteering can do nothing but help. Just allocate your time accordingly and make sure you don't start volunteering all of over the place hoping that will lead somewhere. Target these opportunities the same way you would a job. Section 6

10. *Where should I go to meet people in my industry?*
    See the networking section of this book – I go into great detail on this. Section 5

11. *Should I go back to school?*

It depends. If you know that you will eventually need an MBA and you want to add sustainability, then by all means. But I caution people because they hope that by going through school, they'll be assisted by their institution to help them land their dream job, when the reality is that most career services centers may not have a person familiar with your field. Look at online classes, workshops, even certifications and trainings from groups like ISSP. Section 2

12. *Who should I talk to?*

The networking section has a few worksheets that will help you figure this out. Section 5

13. *What should I follow online?*

Put a Google Alert on the types of things you want to check out. That way every day things are delivered to your inbox about the industries and companies you want to check out. Then go to your Twitter account or set one up and follow industry thought leaders and the companies you are interested in. Section 5

14. *Should I hire a Recruiter?*

Unless you are already a Sustainability Manager or have the title above that, the answer is a definite NO. Recruiters in general don't 'get' sustainability. You may find one that does, but that would be an exception. Pass on the recruiter. Section 5

SECTION 1: WHO ARE YOU AND WHAT DO YOU WANT

"You don't know where you are going, unless you know where you are!" - Old Sailing Metaphor

I start with this quote because far too many people jump straight into a job search and start applying for jobs without fully thinking what exactly it is that they are looking for. Depending on where you are in your life, career, relationships and financial needs, each time you start a job search, the situation will be slightly different.

By thinking through your current situation, your limits, your aspirations and your priorities, the job search becomes clearer and you can realistically begin to tackle your next move.

Worksheet 1: Career Planning - Inventory of Needs and Wants
This career planning worksheet is designed to help you do a quick inventory of your needs and wants so that you can put some parameters around your job search. For example, if you are in a very serious relationship and your significant other doesn't want to leave town, then you better factor that into your location search.

I bring this up because a good friend of mine got married right after undergrad and was in the process of applying to graduate school with his wife. They applied all over the country to their top schools, but only had two that overlapped in the same city. When they didn't get into those two schools but still wanted to pursue their careers, this caused problems. It put so much stress on their relationship that they ended up divorcing shortly thereafter.

Go through this worksheet and clearly define what your needs are. If you are just getting started these will be very different than if you are more established in your career. But it is important that you think deeply about these questions and be honest with yourself.

"Know yourself. Understand what you love to do and what you hate to do, what you want to learn, what you want to avoid learning, whether you are a people person, how persistent you are, what types of companies you want to work for, etc. Write it down. This can be hard when you first start your career, but will help you narrow down and focus in on roles that are a good fit for you and know when to pass on applying for a position." Jake Swenson—Director of Sustainability, Staples[i]

A. Life Questions

1. Why are you considering a career or transition into sustainability? (New challenge, values, higher income, bigger role, want ownership, save the planet, etc.)

2. Are you looking for your ideal job in sustainability or a transitional job for a year or two that will position yourself for that ideal job? When do you want to make this career transition? Three months? One year?

3. What do you think you need most at this stage of your career? (Higher salary, flexibility, benefits, mentoring, growth potential, mgmt experience, sustainability experience)

4. What personal things do you have planned over the next two years that you will need to factor in this decision? (Engagement, marriage, move, purchase house or car, kids, other)

5. When do you anticipate this taking place? How will this affect your decision making process?

B. *Location Questions*

1. Where do you want to live and work? (Describe the ideal city, town or community - consider location, jobs in sustainability, outdoor activities, close to water or mountains, commute, size, near family, etc.)

2. Does your current location meet these criteria? Why or why not?

3. What are some places that might fit these criteria? (Portland, Blacksburg, Seattle, Jackson Hole, Boulder) List five places.

C. *Personal Questions*

1. Describe your best strengths.
    What would your co-workers, boss, spouse, significant other and best friends say are your greatest strengths? For example:

    - Analytical skills
    - Communication skills
    - Ability to generate ideas
    - Facilitation
    - Knowledge of the environment or a sustainability background

    - Business development and client relationships
    - Research
    - Writing and editing
    - Public speaking
    - Math/finance skills

"My advice for trying to get any job, including one in sustainability, is to seek positions that maximize your strengths. And I like this equation of Strength. Strength = Talent x (knowledge + skill). In other words, what are you already good at? Where's your talent? Are you a people person? Are you good with numbers? Are you a better idea brainstormer than your friends? There are so many aspects to sustainability that it will be easy to find a role once you identify and begin to build your strength." Dan Stonington—Executive Director, NW Natural Resource Group[ii]

2. Describe your character. How would your friends and the people you care about most describe you? How would your professional colleagues (bosses, co-workers) describe you?

   For example:
   - Passionate about sustainability
   - Attention to detail/quality
   - Loyal
   - Commitment to follow-through
   - Work in fast paced environment

   - Variety of interests
   - Flexible, independent
   - Willingness to learn
   - Positive attitude/ strong work ethic
   - Facilitator of win-win transactions

3. What do you LOVE to do?

4. From a career perspective, in what roles do you best excel?

5. Are the answers to questions three and four the same? Why or why not?

6. Describe the job environment you want to work in.

   For example:
   - Independent work environment
   - Flexible work hours
   - Work/Life balance
   - Product and company I believe in
   - If non-profit: focused on relationship building; development
   - If for-profit: I want to believe in the product and service, focused on results and efficacy

D. Work Questions

1. Why do you want to do this work? Will this work enable you to make the difference in the world that you desire?

   "Determine what change you would like to bring about in the world and some of the applied ways you can do this." Cynthia Figge—Co-Founder and COO, CSR Hub[iii]

2. What do you want to do on a day to day basis? Describe the work and the content of what you do. For example:

   - Research
   - Writing
   - Data Analytics
   - Carbon Inventories

3. What do you NOT want to do? Think of both the work environment and content. For example:

   - Corporate or 9-5
   - Full time desk job
   - Non-profit: fundraising and grant writing
   - Compromise my values
   - Deal with office politics
   - Sales/asking for money
   - Long commute

4. What industry are you interested in? For example: Clean Technology, Energy, Green Building, Consulting, Aquatic Ecology, etc.

5. Within this industry, what specific types of companies are you looking at? For example in the Clean Technology industry: wind, solar, biodiesel, smart grid, etc.

6. Have you seen any jobs posted that you are interested in? If so, where? Which companies?

7. If not, how could you create this job? (Start your own business, get two part-time jobs, find a way to incorporate into my existing job)

8. What type of compensation and benefits are you looking for? What is the MINIMAL that you could make and be happy? Break these down individually but start first with salary, then benefits.

9. If you need to transition, what are some jobs (either full-time or part-time) that you could do as intermediate steps to better position yourself for your desired job? What other things (volunteer, board, training, etc.) do you need to do between now and then to make yourself more marketable?

10. When trying to choose between careers or job opportunities, answer these three questions:
    a. What will help you get to where you want to be?
    b. How much money do you need?
    c. How will this affect your life-work balance?

11. Create an elevator pitch explaining why you are the right person for the job. To start, come up with a few descriptors, like the ones below, and then build your pitch:
    - Worked in sustainability. understand the industry, marketplace, and demand
    - Dual degree: environmental Studies/Business
    - Strong CSR Researcher
    - Good with people, sales, client relationships, communication
    - Understand why consumers make decisions (individual/business)
    - Enjoy business development, sales, and building client relationships

    Here is an example using those descriptors:
    "Experienced CSR professional looking for a business development role where I can help a company increase sales and build client relationships by truly understanding why its customers choose their sustainability products or services."

12. List your network and the first people you want to meet with. Be specific in who they are, your connection, how you will connect with them and their contact information.

    - Whose opinion do you most respect? (Teacher, friend's parent who's successful, etc.)
    - Where have you made your most positive impact? (School, work, place of worship, volunteer)
    - Who's most inclined to help you? (Family, friends, boss, other)
    - Who are connectors? (People that know everyone – natural networkers you should connect to)

    See the worksheet below to help you get a basic start on identifying your networks. Section 3 then provides a more comprehensive approach to building your network.

Worksheet 2: Identifying Your Networks

This chart is an example of identifying and organizing your network.

Who	Connection	How to Connect with them?	Contact Info (phone/email)
Professional			
Dave Smith	Former Boss	Don't have info, will look on LinkedIn	TBD
Shirley Adams	Co-worker (former)	Call Stacy, she will have Shirley's info	stacy@gmail.com
John Mann	My Banker	Ask him to do coffee next time I'm in the bank	310-555-1212
Family Friends			
Jenn's Mom	Best friend Jenn's mom who knows everyone in outdoor retail industry	Send Facebook message to Jenn	Facebook Messenger
Tim's Dad	Very networked in the sustainability field	Will see Tim on Friday, ask for e-intro	858-555-1212
Professors			
Prof. Davis	Encouraged me on my path	Call school's info line and get his office number	TBD
Prof. William	Has been a reference for me before	Email and ask if I can chat with her for 10-15 minutes	william@university.edu
Green Drinks Contacts			
Jessie Johnson	Met at the last event, knows several people at companies I'm interested in	IM with her on Facebook	Facebook Messenger

Instructions:

This exercise will enable you to highlight the top people in each category for you to reach out to.

Complete the worksheet below. Be sure to put the name, organization, and email/phone contact information for each person.

Who	Connection	How to Connect with them?	Contact Info (phone/email)
Professional			
Family Friends			
Professors, College or Graduate School Contacts			
Green Drinks or Professional Network Contacts			
Other			

Identifying Your Next Step

Now that you've gotten clarity on your strengths, what it is that you really want, and have begun to organize your list of contacts, it's time to explore the different potential routes to landing that dream green job. Your job search will likely not be as simple as going straight from A to B. Depending upon where you are in your career and level of experience, there will be multiple paths to get there, some of which I'll explain below.

This graphic below shows several different paths towards your desired job:

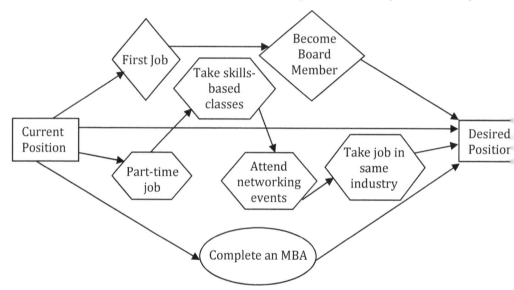

Rectangle Path: This process is a straight path from your current position to your desired job. This is of course what everyone wants, but is atypical in this field. This is only likely if you are established and have years of experience in the field.

Hexagon Path: This is the most likely scenario, especially if you are just starting out. You may have to take a part-time job in order to be able to take classes and attend workshops to round out your skill set. In addition, you might have to attend specific networking events before finding a job in the industry you want to work in. By doing all of this work, it eventually leads to your desired job.

Diamond Path: Sometimes the path is not as clear cut as one would anticipate. In fact, almost all of us in the field have had some weird steps from where we were to where we are today, including me. It might make more sense to take a lesser job or one that is out of the sustainability field to pay the bills and build your network. In this example you take a job, then find an organization where you can become a board member to round out your resume and this helps lead to a connection to your dream job.

Oval Path: This path means that maybe you need to go back to school for a sustainability MBA, Certificate, or any type of schooling that not only builds your skill set, but your network as well. Maybe you go part-time or take a complete break from the workforce, go back to school and then come out armed with what you need to land your dream job.

"You may need endurance and commitment. Getting that first job out of college isn't always easy. Can't find the perfect dream job on day one? Don't despair and don't give up. Be willing to work seasonal or short term jobs, try volunteering for sustainability organizations, keep networking, and take classes on the side to build key knowledge and skills. Sometimes it takes working a job unrelated to sustainability to pay the bills while building your sustainability resume in the evenings or on the weekends. You never know when you might be in the right place at the right time for your big break." Jo Opdyke Wilhelm—Senior Ecologist, King County Water and Land Resources Division[iv]

Tips to Better Position Yourself for Your Next Step

If you don't feel 100% qualified for the job you want, don't worry. You are not alone. Below are some examples for ways to attain additional experience that can better qualify you for that desired job.

- Try to incorporate sustainability into your existing job or join a 'green team' inside your company.

"Implement a sustainability program at your current job. For example you might set up a composting program or convince the Marketing department to switch to 100% recycled paper or something like that. This will also allow you to demonstrate that you have what it takes." Jackie Drumheller— Sustainability Manager, Alaska Airlines[v]

If you are a student, remember that you are paying for your education, so use your classes to your advantage.
- If you have a finance or accounting class, see if you can do a case study about a company that has saved money by going green
- If you are in a strategy class, see if you can help a firm develop their sustainability strategy
- If it's a marketing class, see if you can help a firm create their marketing strategy around sustainability

If you are currently in a job:
- Check out whatever has been done at your firm and identify what else can be done
- Join the green team
- Talk to people who have been involved and interested in this, and see if you can take on a project or two inside the firm

"I tell people to look where they are. If they are currently in a role in their company, they should look to find a way to develop some sustainability work there. If that company isn't already integrating sustainability principles, then they need a leader like that 30/40 something to make it happen." Brenna Davis—Director of Sustainability, Virginia Mason/ Chair, WBCA[vi]

- Try part-time (PT) work if full-time (FT) work is unavailable. The hidden secret is that most people working in sustainability used to do it in the evenings or on weekends when they were getting started. Don't be afraid to take a PT job that has to do with sustainability. Try to look for a job within the industry or company that you want to work for. This will better position you in the future to get your desired role.

  "Be willing to do projects, internships, jobs for free initially. Do something, anything to build your resume in the area you eventually want a job in. Find opportunities - or even create them - to build skills that will be useful to future positions." Sean Schmidt—Office of Sustainability Assistant Director of Communications & Programs, University of Washington[vii]

- Volunteer with local non-profits or businesses. Consider checking the list of companies from your Chamber of Commerce, the Chinook Book, the Blue-Green Guide, and Earth Share.

  "Join working groups or volunteer groups addressing sustainability within your desired industry to get experience, make contacts and to better understand the industry." Matt O'Laughlin— Sustainability Manager, K2 Sports[viii]

- Sit on boards of companies or non-profits that can provide you with experience or credibility. This is a great way to learn the lingo of the industry and to meet contacts.

- Enroll in an online sustainability program, where coursework and opportunities to work with local businesses overlap.

  "Educate yourself; if your institution does not provide programs or courses in sustainability, and then seek online programs, certificates or continuing education learning modules to help you build your knowledge base. When possible, seek courses that provide experiential learning that directly connect you to real projects within your communities." Marianella Franklin—Chief Sustainability Officer, University of Texas Rio-Grande Valley[ix]

- When inquiring with a business or an individual about job opportunities, be specific. This is important not only for getting the most useful information, but also in terms of etiquette. E.g. "I have an interest in X, Y, and Z - where should I research that topic?"

- If you are trying to build out your resume, remember, if you take two PT jobs, each somewhat related to sustainability, you may actually better position yourself for your dream job than if you just took one FT. When you get done with the two PT's, you'll have two different perspectives and experiences to talk about. And, say you have four noteworthy accomplishments for each of the PT jobs, now you have eight bullet points on your resume. Add a few volunteer gigs and you're at 10!

- Break up the job search. It's easy to get stuck in a rut when searching, and let's face it, searching for a job isn't fun. Find ways to break it up. Find part-time work to help break up the day. If you work two and a half days a week, that'll help you focus your time and efforts those other two and a half days. This will allow you to set aside specific times when you can network and research, plus it'll help you feel like you are doing something while you search for a better fit. Moreover, when you are talking with people instead of saying you are "Unemployed, between jobs, or looking for work" you can say, "Currently I'm working part-time at 'X' but what I'm hoping to do is 'Y.'"

SECTION 2: EXPLORING YOUR OPTIONS

Anytime I meet with someone trying to break into this space, they ask, *"Other than being a CSR Manager or Sustainability Consultant, what other jobs are out there?"*

The answer is that there are sustainability jobs everywhere, and in almost every discipline. In fact there are probably 50x more jobs in traditional disciplines that can also incorporate sustainability than there are pure sustainability jobs. For example, there are way more jobs in traditional roles (such as marketing, supply chain, facilities, and logistics) that need a person with sustainability expertise than there are CSR/Sustainability Manager positions.

"Take a broad view of what a 'job in sustainability' means. Know that there are not that many positions with 'sustainability' in their title. Almost any job in a core function can incorporate sustainability." Sarah Martinez—Sustainability Maven, Eco Products[x]

Expand Your Horizon - Looking Beyond CSR Sustainability Roles

What I tell people is to first figure out how to line up their skills (what are they good at?) and then layer sustainability into that role. So if you are good at accounting, finance, marketing, supply chain, community outreach, or communications, find a way to bring sustainability into your discipline. Your knowledge of sustainability will be your differentiator in those fields!

"Look to fully explore the possibilities of expanding your work in your current role/company. If you've been in a specific industry for a while, you're an expert there. You will be better positioned to find opportunities for improvement/change in your industry than those from the outside." Janice Lichtenwaldt—Sr. Mgr IT Communications, T-Mobile[xi]

In many ways, sustainability jobs are in the same trajectory as how e-commerce jobs were about 15 years ago. Eventually, e-commerce became business as usual and is no longer viewed as a standalone skill, which is the same with sustainability jobs. In about five to ten years, these specific 'sustainability jobs' will go away because it'll just be part of how people do their jobs.

"My impression is that for the next five years +/- it's more like an added skill set that is going to be a differentiator for someone who wants a 'real job' in operations, product development, procurement, real estate, etc...and then after that, it's going to be table stakes to be qualified for a job in those areas." Kevin Hagen—CSR Director, Iron Mountain[xii]

Here are some ways to incorporate sustainability into your existing job:

Department/Job	Ways to Incorporate Sustainability
Accounting	Tracking environmental, greenhouse gas and financial performance
Finance	Managing investments could include Socially Responsible Investing options
Marketing	Reaching out to green consumers or 'Lifestyle Of Health and Sustainability' (LOHAS) customers
Public Relations	Creating positive stories about your sustainability efforts
Supply Chain & Logistics	Tracking the sustainability and financial performance of your supply chain
Human Resources	Using sustainability to attract millennials, new talent and improve retention
Legal/Risk Mgmt	Including climate, environmental and social categories into your risk management and resiliency planning
Facilities	Identifying ways the company can save money by reducing energy, water & waste costs

Here are some ways to capitalize on your background and incorporate sustainability into your existing job that are typically not thought of as 'sustainability jobs:'

Department/Job	Ways to Incorporate Sustainability
Chemistry	Look at non-toxic chemical alternatives, chemicals on the restricted substance list, green chemistry options
Engineering	Learn how to conduct a Life Cycle Analysis (LCA), or how to manage a building more efficiently from an energy and cost perspective
Arts/Music	Teach about expression of social justice through song and art
Political Science	Research public policies and their impact on the environment, community and business
Communications	Learn about external reporting requirements from groups such as investors, donors, CDP and GRI, and help your firm in this regard
Agriculture	Incorporate sustainable practices such as organic, Global Gap, Salmon Safe, and Fair Trade into how the land is farmed
Humanities/Social Sciences	Help your firm answer value chain questionnaires on human rights, worker conditions, etc.
Psychology	Provide trainings on the importance of understanding personal & organizational behavior when trying to make change

Create Your Own Position

There is definitely an entrepreneurial aspect to finding a job in sustainability, and for many people, the idea of being 'entrepreneurial' may seem foreign, and you might be thinking to yourself, "That's not me!" I was the same way, in that I didn't think of myself as creative or as a particularly entrepreneurial person, so don't despair if you are feeling like I did.

The reality is that because you aren't just trying to find any job, but a job in sustainability, you may end up having to create your own job. The organization you are working for may not have a full-time sustainability position, or your dream company may already have a person in that role, and you may need to get creative on how you can add value to their company.

If you think that the idea of creating your own job is crazy, remember that there have been _THREE sequels_ to the movie _Sharknado_!"

For many people, a sustainability position often starts as part-time or half-time, but once they are able to demonstrate business value and show both the risks and opportunities that an organization is facing, then eventually the organization puts whoever is in this role (and this could be you) into the full-time position.

I know a colleague who was serving as the International Sales Director as his full-time job when his organization received a questionnaire from a major customer about climate change. Prior to his work there, the colleague had attended a sustainability focused graduate school, so his boss asked him to handle the situation as they were unsure who else to give it to. He helped answer this customer request and by doing so, was able to show his company that it needed someone dedicated to this role even if it was only part-time to start. As the requests increased, it became evident that this role was important enough that it needed a full-time position and since he had proven himself, they handed him the job.

Know Your Numbers and Be Able to Make the Business Case

Finally, no matter which route you take or position you strive for, you must be able to make the business case for sustainability. No matter if you find a job as a Sustainability/CSR Manager, you create your own position, or you are trying to incorporate it into an existing or traditional role, you need to back up your ideas, suggestions or arguments with hard numbers.

When pitching an idea, the following ideas will not fly: "It's the right thing to do," "It's part of our culture," or "It will help with our brand value and employee recruiting." While all of these statements are correct, the reality is that while important, most decision makers will expect you to come to the table with hard numbers and case studies from other companies that back up your claims and show a path to success.

Therefore, if you are looking to incorporate sustainability into a role, be sure to instead say, "If we implement 'X,' which will require $5,000, then we can not only save energy and reduce GHG emissions, but it will have an ROI of 10% within a two year period." Then if you can back this up with a similar company in your industry as a case study, you will have strengthened your argument.

The same is true with how you talk about sustainability whether in a networking situation or by putting successes on your resume (which I talk about in the next section), you need to know the numbers and make the business case for sustainability.

SECTION 3: TARGET YOUR JOB SEARCH

Now that you've inventoried who you are, your skills, and the specifics as to what you are looking for, it's time to target your job search.

Most job seekers get started by just Googling job sites and applying or by randomly sending emails out to friends stating, "If you know anyone that might be looking for someone, let me know!" This is called the Fire-Ready-Aim approach and, unfortunately, it often does not work.

What you need to do is take the time to target your job search and tailor your message to each company. Ready-Aim-Fire. This can take time and can be tedious, but it is also one of the most important aspects of your job search.

Narrowing Your Job Search

Typically, there are two ways people search for jobs:

A. The 'gunshot' approach:
    Apply for any and all potential jobs that you might be interested in

B. The 'rifle' approach:
    Apply for the specific job and organization you want

A. *The 'Gunshot' Approach*
This approach is where you send out your resume to every company and every position that you are even remotely interested in. You are basically shooting a bunch of scatter shots into the world and hoping you'll hit something. Unfortunately, for the jobs you are looking for, this will never, ever work.

B. *The 'Rifle' Approach*
The rifle approach involves opening and closing doors. In order to converge on the exact job for you, first you have to consider all of the possibilities and then start closing some doors to narrow your search.

Let's go through an example following the 'rifle' approach to determine what your ideal job position would be. Your starting point is:

"I want a job in Clean Technology, something exciting that helps solve climate change."

Step 1: First determine the industries in the clean tech space.

- Solar
- **Wind**
- Micro-Hydro
- Biomass
- Tidal
- Co-Generation
- Methane Recapture
- Biofuels

Step 2: Next, after researching those different industries, you determine that your key area of interest is wind. Digging deeper, you identify the different types of companies in the wind sector:

- **Wind Power Consultants**
- Turbine manufacturers
- Sighting consultants
- Distributors
- Wind farm construction companies
- Farms interested in wind power
- Local utilities
- Distributed Generation firms
- Transmission companies

Clean Tech Example:

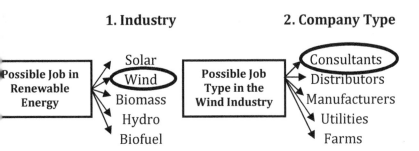

Step 3: From that list, you determine that the most important thing to you is finding a wind power business that not only shares your values, but is in a place you'd actually want to live. As part of your research, determine locations that work for you:

Locations:
- **Seattle**
- Austin
- Portland
- New York City
- San Francisco
- St. Paul/Minneapolis

Step 4: Now that you've determined where you want to work, take into consideration what you want to do, your existing skills and experience, and narrow this down to your ideal role:

- **Marketing**
- Research & Development
- Communications
- Finance/Accounting
- Management
- Sales/Outreach

Step 5: Taking all of this research into account, now create your elevator pitch. The key to a great elevator pitch is keeping it short, to the point and something that the person on the other end can not only remember, but is able to repeat when they introduce you to others. This last part is very important.

In this example, your elevator pitch might be:
"I want to work for a wind power consultancy that shares my values, in a marketing role, and is located in Seattle area."

Go ahead and write yours down on a piece of paper or type it up. What is your elevator pitch? Don't worry if this takes you a while. It might take multiple attempts.

For example, it recently took me weeks to land on mine, which is: "I'm one of the world's leading consultants and teachers in the field of sustainability. I look for opportunities to help organizations increase profitability, enhance their brand value and reduce risk through better social & environmental practices."

Worksheet 3: Narrowing Your Job Search

After you have created your elevator pitch, it's time to get specific on your search. Use the worksheet below to first identify the types of industries that you are interested in and then the companies. When you complete this worksheet, you will have gotten much more specific in your job search which will make the whole process easier.

Industries	Types of Companies	Locations	Potential Roles	Target Companies

Tips for your search

How do you find the companies and the positions you are looking for? Below are a few tips for getting started:

1. **Create a job search keyword list**
   - Make a list of search keywords that relate to your goals. For example, using phrases such as 'public relations,' 'social justice' and 'business' will help you find opportunities in socially conscious companies within the marketing/PR department
   - Use them when searching LinkedIn job openings (then filter based on location and experience level)
   - Search for jobs by titles, if you know the exact role you want

2. *Build your job search around companies*
   - 'Follow' companies and organizations you have been eyeing on LinkedIn and Twitter
   - Join company and career-related groups so you don't miss out on recruitment news
   - Set Google Alerts on these key words so stories are delivered directly to your inbox

3. *Find the right contacts*
   - Learn the titles and/or names of key target contacts
   - Enter the company's email suffix in a search engine. This will hopefully lead you to the full email address of an employee who works at the firm. For example '@XYZcorp.com.'
   - Look for industry peers to connect with and brainstorm a list of industry leaders as potential targets. Use LinkedIn's Company Search function to locate the companies within your target industry and narrow down by geography, company size, and your relationship to that company
   - Check out 'Best Of' lists produced by associations and publishing companies, such as Society of Human Resource Management, Puget Sound Business Journal, Fortune, etc.
   - Do a zip code search using LinkedIn's Company Search function (you can sort by industry, company size and more) then assemble a list of employers in your area

Managing the Process

Oftentimes job seekers are overwhelmed by the variety of different opportunities that exist. There are so many that they just don't know what to focus on or what skill sets to prioritize. So instead they start volunteering and talking to just about anyone – even if they are on the fringes of what they are interested in. This isn't the right way.

>   *Step 1:* First identify your dream position (what type of firm, what are the characteristics, your preferred role, salary, location, etc.). As an example, your dream position could be, "I want a position that is doing 'X,' I want to be mentored, I want growth potential, and I want a salary earning 'Y' and I want to do this by the middle of next year." Once you have identified your goal, then you can work backwards to the present day.

>   *Step 2:* Take an inventory of your current skill set, experience, etc. and talk to people in your dream position. Look at job postings and qualification requirements so that you can identify gaps that you need to take care of.

>   *Step 3:* Once you have identified your gaps, start working on how best to gain the experience and knowledge that you need.

For example: Your goal is above in Step 1, but after further analysis you've identified the following gaps in your skill set: you need a Certificate in Sustainability, you need three years of experience in the field (you only have two), and you need a firm understanding of carbon credit markets. Now you know what you don't know and can take steps to gain that experience.

Worksheet 4: Your Process and Timeline

Now that you've identified your gaps, the next step is to develop a plan and timeline. People often get overwhelmed because they think they need to do it all at once, which isn't the case. Instead, break it up into bite size chunks and realize that there is no magic formula. It just helps to be realistic about what you need to do and how long this may take. This will also help you keep yourself accountable and allow you to benchmark your progress as you juggle day-to-day priorities. Below is an example of what that might look like:

	Short Term (1-3 Months)	Medium Term (4-6 Months)	Long Term (6-9 Months)
Areas To Focus On	• Network • Talk to people in the industry • Find out what qualifications are needed • Figure out the firms you want to look at • Apply to a certificate program	• Volunteer or take a part-time job for an org. that is working on Wind • Find reasons to start networking with your dream company	• Get nominated to the board of the organization that does the carbon credits • Start networking for dream job • Volunteer at the dream company
Skills Needed	• Gain experience in carbon markets, carbon footprinting, CSR, and finance	• Attend carbon credit/market conference • Go to a workshop on this topic	• Get certified in carbon credits and offsets for the wind industry
Where to Get it	• Enroll in an International Society for Sustainability Professionals certificate course	• Take certificate course	• Graduate with certificate

Use the example from the previous chart and fill in your own timeline. If your timeline is shorter, then go ahead and adjust the timing across the top to whatever you need. It might be Month 1, Month 2 and Months 3-4, whatever your timing is. However if you are looking to make a major career change, then the one below is more likely. If you are a college senior, then maybe break it down by quarter or month. Be sure to factor in finances and be honest about how long it will take while not neglecting your personal responsibilities (family, relationships, friends, etc.).

	Short Term (1-3 Months)	Medium Term (4-6 Months)	Long Term (6-9 Months)
Areas To Focus On			
Skills Needed			
Where to Get it			

"Where is your money going to come from? Do you have a back-up financial plan? Can a partner support you for a while? Have part-time skills? If you're pursuing work for a values-based reason it will be easier and more impactful if you can go all in without worrying about where the money is coming from at first. A lot of us are in jobs we don't like because of a long list of compromises that we made for lots of good reasons. But now you're tired of compromising. So don't. But before you do, make sure you can pay your bills, or downsize until you can pay your bills." Derek Eisel—Director of Sales, Scope 5[xiii]

Worksheet 5: Breaking Up Your Job Search Schedule

How do you schedule time to look for a job if you are currently working? When should you do it if you are in school?

It is going to be different for everyone, but the most important thing is that you block off times on your calendar, just like you would anything else of importance and commit to those dates and times. You'll be far more effective if you do this than if you just haphazardly look for work, because more than likely, you'll find something else that you'd rather be doing than looking for a job.

The biggest myth is that 'looking for a job is a full-time job.' The reality is that in any given day, you cannot commit eight hours straight into your job search. Maybe for the first few days or two weeks, but soon you'll begin to have diminishing returns and you'll lose energy. It's similar to working on your computer. If you do nothing but that all day, every day, you'll find yourself day dreaming, searching the web for other things, etc. So depending on if you are unemployed, still in school or working already, take a look at your week and plan out when you are going to allocate specific time for your job search. Note that the AM/PM times don't mean you have to allocate all four hours, but maybe you just allocate an hour during your lunch, or when you have a break in your day. But do get specific, make a plan, write it down and be disciplined enough to follow it.

Your Schedule	Mon	Tue	Wed	Thurs	Fri	Sat	Sun
8-12 AM							
Lunch							
1-5 PM							
Evening							

SECTION 4: TAILOR YOUR RESUME

Everyone has a resume. Unfortunately, most of our resumes are out of date and don't do a very good job of telling the person on the other end who we truly are, what our best assets are and how we can help them. We've been taught that we should put our education at the top and then have our experience flow in chronological order. This is dated, and if you are applying for a job, you need to consider the tips below and update your resume.

Remember, the resume isn't about you. It's about the person on the other end. They have a role that they need filled and they are wondering if you are the right person for the job. They have specific wants and needs, and it's your job to tailor your resume to meet their descriptions and requirements. Be authentic, definitely don't make anything up or oversell yourself, but you have to put yourself in the other person's shoes who is thinking, "Why am I looking at this person's resume?"

In addition, attention spans are much shorter than they used to be. For example, in our office, when looking at resumes, we generally spend less than five seconds per resume. If someone doesn't have it tailored and it isn't easy to understand how they can meet our needs, we hit delete or toss their resume into the recycling bin. In these cases their cover letter and references won't even get looked at.

Food Analogy: I'll liken your resume to ordering food. If someone is looking for a vegetarian meal and they tell you so, your first thought would not be to show them all the meat options, seafood options, desserts, and surf & turf specials first. You'll want to show them the vegetarian options first, then you can go ahead and list the other food options.

The same is true with your resume; you have to tailor it to the reader on the other end and what *they* care about.

The Secret of the Three Yeses

In order to get the interviewer or hiring manager to read beyond the first few paragraphs and to truly engage with your resume, you want them to say, "Yes" three times in the first 5-10 seconds of reading your resume.

How do you do this? It's easy and only requires three steps:

1. *Tailor your personal statement (as best you can) to the job description*
   For example, if they are looking for 'an independent, self starter to run a company's green team,' then you need to highlight how you meet that qualification. Or, if they are looking for someone who is 'an excellent communicator to perform marketing and community outreach,' then you'll need to talk about your skills in that area. If you do that, you have accomplished Yes #1.

2. *Tailor your skills*
   Most job descriptions list out specific skills that they are seeking or familiarity with various programs. Therefore, make sure to match your skills to what they are looking for (if you have them). Keep your skills to your best ones and no more than six. I can't tell you how many times someone has disqualified themselves by listing eight, nine, or ten skills. This basically says that they don't have any core skills or didn't take the time to evaluate their fit for this role. Less is more here. Match what they are looking for, if you do this, that leads to Yes #2.

3. *Ditch the chronological resume and put your related experience at the top*
   I mentioned this earlier but I can't underscore this enough. Ditch the chronological order. That is old, tired and very 1990's. If attention spans are 5-10 seconds, you'll want to put your best foot forward as soon as you can.

How do you do this? Break your experience into 'Related Experience' and 'Other Experience.' That way you can highlight all the sustainability experience that relates to what they are looking for at the top. Go ahead and put your best, most applicable experience for this job here whether it is project work, school related, volunteer or board. The important thing is that you'll want to demonstrate that you have what it takes for THIS role, so put your related experience at the top and then the rest under 'Other Experience.' This gets you to Yes #3.

Realize that if the reader likes your experience related to this position, then they will read on and see what else you have done, where you went to school, hobbies, etc., but if you just list everything chronologically because you've had a variety of different jobs, this ends up putting the burden on the reader to try and figure out how you might fit into this position.

Don't be lazy. Take the extra 10 minutes EVERY time you are sending a resume to a person, even if only for an informational interview. If there is a job description or it's a company that you are interested in, tailor it to the conversation you are having. Help yourself by helping the other person to understand quickly and easily who you are, and remember to try and get them to say "Yes" three times in the first three aspects of your resume.

"I look to see how well the person writes and conveys their qualifications and connects their hopes and dreams with the real needs of the job. And make sure the cover letter is personal and heartfelt. We are changing the world right? Take the time to do it right." Cynthia Figge—Co-Founder and COO, CSR Hub[xiv]

General Tips

- The top third of the page of your resume is the most important. Most reviewers won't even bother to read beyond a half page, so don't save your best for last. Put your key goals and job-related skills in a statement at the top

- Move the education section to the bottom – people will look down there anyway to see where you went to school

- Describe your achievements in a concise and measurable way, ex. "Helped the company save $25,000 in operations." Don't just make a list of things you have done. Show numbers

> *"An individual needs to walk two different worlds: the traditional business environment and the sustainable community. Being able to create value enhancing linkages is the key whether this is identified as a cost savings initiative, a return on capital, improvement in efficiency or safety (risk reduction)." Patrick Drum— Portfolio Manager & Research Analyst, Saturna Capital*[xv]

- Don't talk about your passion for the environment. Everyone has that. And that doesn't help them with the position unless it's an environmental activist position like working for the U.S. Public Interest Research Group

> *"Being an 'enviro' is not a qualification for a job, I'm not even sure it's an asset." Jeremy King— Campus Sustainability Coordinator, Denison University*[xvi]

- Combine your accomplishments with your work. Don't put too many bullets for each job, three or four is best

- Club involvement (from college) is not very important. Instead show what you did through volunteering

"On a resume, I look for communication skills, change management, understanding of sustainability issues, and community involvement on environmental issues through volunteering." Brenna Davis—Director of Sustainability, Virginia Mason/ Chair, WBCA[xvii]

- Make sure that you don't start each sentence with the same verb. Mix it up. For example if you currently have 'Delivered' in your first four bullets, change it to 'Delivered, Monitored, Prepared, and Coordinated'

- With education, put your most recent degree first and work backwards. Be sure you use the same tense throughout. Things that don't apply, remove. Don't write 'Related Coursework.' Nothing screams lack of experience than simply stating that you 'took this in school'

- Think through each job you're applying for and ask yourself, "What will they really care about?" Focus on this particular job, whether it is management, programming, research, marketing, etc.

"Be sure to tailor your skills, background, and messaging for each application - a generic resume and cover letter stick out like a sore thumb and signals a lack of interest and attention to detail." Jo Opdyke Wilhelm— Senior Ecologist, King County Waste and Land Resources Division[xviii]

- Have a master version of your resume that you can tailor based on the audience you are giving it to. For example, if you are generalist, have your sustainability resume, and then a second or third one that focuses on a particular skill (public relations) or industry (outdoor recreation). By having a master, you can put everything in one place and then pull from it as needed

- Keep a personal portfolio of everything you've done and achieved as well as your skills and interests

- At the bottom of your resume include something that is unique and tells the interviewer about who you are

"I also look for interesting things about them that I might leverage in creative ways. Are they an outdoors person; perhaps I can have them work with an outdoor industry client in a new way. Once I assess a candidate is qualified or close to it, I am less concerned with the details of work experience and more concerned with fit, energy and resilience. I welcome a person with non-traditional backgrounds. It is something that has worked well in many projects." Claudia Capitini—Founder and Principal, Maven Consulting, LLC[xix]

Example of a Good Resume

Name, Title

Profile
"Name" has over 4 years of consulting experience in delivering sustainability strategies and cost savings to organizations in the outdoor and tourism industries that is looking to bring my sustainability, analytical, and communication skills to the role of "A" and organization "B"

Key Strengths
- Sustainability and Business Strategy
- Financial/Cost Savings Analytics
- Sustainability Implementation and Planning
- Excellent writer, strong presentation skills
- Business development and lead generation
- Professional Facil

Professional Experience
Environmental Consulting Company X   *2016 – Present*
Junior Consultant
- Calculated and led 2 different clients through successful GHG reporting processes and helped both identify reduction strategies
- Increased company's lead generation in the sustainability space by 150% in just 3 years on only a $10,000 budget
- Managed my company's green team of 15 members. Identified and implemented 30 cost saving and environmentally beneficial ideas
- Facilitated and then delivered executive-level sustainability master plan and strategy to the company Board

Business Consulting Company Y   2014–2016
Associate
- Was the project manager during a restructuring of an eco-tourism client that turn a $180,000 loss into a $50,000 profit in two years
- Led the creation of the company's first sustainability vision and goals. Created strategic plan and uncovered $30,000 in cost savings

Water Savers Alliance   2013-2015
Volunteer
- Led organization's internal sustainability efforts as a 3 hour a week volunteer with no budget
- Assisted Exec. Director in writing grant that increased program funding by $100,000 and enabled organization to double outreach

Civic Leadership & Community Involvement
- Board Member: Habitat for Humanity
- Member: Young Professionals Network
- Volunteer: Go Green Conference
- Former Chair: Net Impact at "Blank" University

2016 – Present
Present
2014-2015
2013 – 2014

Education
Washington University   Bachelor of Arts   2014
Business and Environmental Studies Double Major   GPA 3.6/4
Extracurricular activities included:
- 4 year college soccer player. Captain my junior and senior season
- Social Justice Community Council Treasure. Company lead school dance troupe that performed over 5 televised performances

Resume "Don'ts"

In addition, there are a number of things that you DON'T want to put on your resume:

- "Passion to save the planet." Yawn, you and everyone else.

  "Assume the person already knows about your passion or principles relative to sustainability or doesn't really care. Don't use precious time communicating them in more than one sentence." Jon Kroman—CEO, Kroman Law[xx]

- "I love animals" and "Enjoy spending time with friends." For the most part, employers assume that about most people. If you put something on there as a differentiator, make it about a hobby, a sport you play, or something that is different.

- "Responsibilities included." Employers don't want to know what your role was, they want to know how you performed in your job and what the results were.

- "Wacky emails." Don't use an email handle such as 'senorwilhelm2009@hotmail.com' as your professional email. Get one with your first and last name. If you have to, create a new one through Gmail or another provider!

Example of a Bad Resume

John Doe

JDoe21@gmail.com   555-555-5555

Objective

Entry level position where I can utilize my Sustainability education to help companies become more sustainable and efficient.

Education

Western University: Bachelor of Science in Sustainability   Graduation 2013

Took over 104 related credits with cumulative GPA: 3.37   Coursework included:

- Business and Sustainability
- Environmental Systems
- Policy and Governance in Biological Systems
- Economics
- Renewable Energy Technologies
- Sustainable Cities
- Urban Planning
- International Development and Sustainability

Experience

- **Customer Ambassador for Monster USA**
  - Performed sales and marketing, customer service, tax and energy reba
  - Supported home energy consulting to residential and commercial clien
  - Direct customer interface on sustainability programs
- **Senior Capstone Project with Professor James Stevens, PhD   2014-2015**
  - 50 year future energy projection final project
  - Was part of a team that developed a plan an energy implementation plan for my professor's side business
- **University Sustainable Apartments Project   2013**
  - Conducted various meeting with tenants about how they could "green" up their apartments
  - Researched sustainable components for an apartment building for my University
- **Restaurant, Pantry and Oven cook**
  - Cooked food for customers
  - Stocked pantry
- **Sustainability Internship: Professor Assistant**
  - Exposure to policy development in business
  - Organized and attended a stakeholder meeting discussing Clean Energy programs in cities

Other

- Enjoy spending time with friends and family
- Enjoys food, wine and good beer
- Loves pets, especially anytime I can play with my cats

Example of a Bad Cover Letter

Dear Honorable Sir/Lady,

Thank you first, for sparing your busy time to look up my application materials. I am an undergraduate student at the University of 'X,' majoring in statistics and economics. At this moment, I am applying for graduate school in finance field for fall of 2018. I desire to gather more experience before I graduate my education. Past education in statistics has equipped me with critical thinking and economics has helped me to combine statistical results with real application. I looked through the duties of this position and I think I can handle it. And more importantly, I am sure I can learn more from this experience. Considering my past experiences and qualifications, I deliver this resume to you prudently, and hope to get a chance to participate in your further interview to show my individual ability to you. If being lucky to get internship with your company, I will certainly grow with the development of your company and make self contribution maximally.

This is not the cover letter you want to write. Here are some reasons why:

1. First of all, it is not addressed to anyone specifically. I get these all the time. They come to my email and don't even have my name, so I don't read any further. I delete it immediately.

2. It is next to impossible to read it because it is one long paragraph. If I'm reading from a mobile device, this just looks like too much work to read. I know that sounds lazy, and it is true. Ask yourself, "Would you read this while studying for a test or cramming to meet a deadline?"

3. In the very second sentence this person (and this was real) already tells me that no matter the role I hire them for, that they are leaving in the fall of 2018. Now this could be okay if this person was applying for a temporary or one year position, but I was looking for someone full-time, and this person has already tipped their hand that they are leaving.

4. They write two things that are bad:
   - "I think I can handle it." Well, people are looking for much more than that in an applicant
   - "More importantly, I can learn from this experience." I'm not hiring for someone to learn from us. I want a candidate to help us and add value, not the other way around

5. Grammar and spelling. If someone has even one spelling or grammar error, they've just shown that they don't have attention to detail and cannot be trusted on communications. Read the last three sentences. This person says, "chance to participate in your further interview…" It gets worse, too. Sorry buddy, I hit delete and never looked at your resume.

Unfortunately, I receive far too many of these. The cover letter is designed to supplement your resume. Yours should highlight particular things you want to mention, fill gaps, and try to convince the reader that if you lack something in one area, other parts of your character will fill that void. Don't be like this person.

Don't be too long. Don't be too wordy. Remember the cover letter should be about the reader and not about what you want to get out of a position. And no matter what, spell and grammar check. Don't eliminate yourself in the first 10 seconds.

SECTION 5: EXECUTION - NETWORKING IS HOW TO GET IT DONE

You've put in the work, now it all comes down to execution. In this section we'll help you take what you've learned and created and help you better brand yourself as you are networking and talking to people about your prospective job.

Most career service centers at Universities and most books don't focus on networking. Instead, they emphasize what they believe to be hard skills, including resume and cover letter writing. Networking is often seen as a "soft skill" that cannot be taught. People believe that you either have it or you don't. I couldn't disagree more; networking is just like any other skill, it can be learned and developed over time. It takes practice, repetition, and most of all, perseverance.

In this section I'm not only going to write about the key points of networking, but will dive deeper into the importance of due diligence, understanding the difference between introverts and extroverts, and the nuances between in-person versus online networking.

Networking is not sleazy
For many people the term networking, just like schmoozing or biz dev, can be a barrier in and of itself. They think it's being sleazy or that you are just trying to sell something. The reality is that networking isn't like that. It's just socializing. Networking is about having conversations, meeting new people, getting to know them and letting them get to know you. It's just the same as talking to a neighbor, a family friend, or someone at the supermarket about what is going on in your work or in your life.

Networking is socializing with a purpose. You want to get to know people, build your network and follow people on social media (LinkedIn, Twitter, etc). In fact, when you follow others and comment on what people are posting online - that's networking.

It is about building relationships

Most people think networking is just about going to events, meeting a bunch of people, gathering a bunch of business cards and then you are done. Wrong! Networking is about building relationships for the long-term where you can help other people and they can hopefully help you. Therefore, one of the most important things about networking is to be authentic. If you are trying to nurture a relationship for the long-term, then being who you truly are is key.

"Be really patient, build a network (including helping others), and assume that something good will happen as the result of something you can't script or envision." Jon Kroman—CEO, Kroman Law[xxi]

Networking - Getting Started

The easiest way to get started is to reach out and network with your friends and people you know.

By starting with people who aren't going to judge you, there's really no risk - if they know someone then they will help you, and if they don't, they'll tell you they don't. A lot of times it's a matter of just getting out there and starting to talk to people because you never know what may come out of it. You could have a conversation with a friend and it turns out that their spouse, colleague, or family member might be the perfect person for you to talk to. Tell people about what you're hoping to do and more than likely they'll try to help you out.

I can't count how many times I have been at social gatherings and when I tell someone I work in sustainability and then ask what they do, my initial thought is, "I don't know if there's going to be a real opportunity for a business connection here, they're not in the sustainability field." But the more we talk and find out about each other, eventually I'll hear, "You know my best friend just mentioned to me that they need help with something along those lines." So the point is, you never know where a solid connection is going to come from. Get clear on what you want, reach out and start talking to people.

Who should I reach out to next?

I tell people to start with individuals whose opinion they most value and respect. Identify that colleague, former boss, or a parent of a friend that seems to have it dialed in. Talk with them and ask for their advice. It may not even be a professional contact – is it a neighbor, teacher or someone at a place of worship whose opinion you most respect? Maybe you've had a few classes where you've really excelled and connected with a specific professor, or you've had a big impact in an extracurricular activity like sports or volunteering. Go and talk to these people and tell them about the job or role you are seeking. Ask them where they think your skills are best utilized, because they've seen you excel. They likely see positive attributes in you that you are blind to, and when they know what you want to do, they will become your cheerleader!

Next, think to yourself, "Who are the connectors?" This seems high school-ish but no matter where you are in life - if you're a 45-year-old in the middle of your career or if you're a 22-year-old just getting her first job - identify your connectors. Think back to high school, "Who were the cool kids?" Who were the people that seemed to know everyone? Now determine who those people are in your industry and in your network.

Key Aspects of Networking

1. Know when to have which conversations

Too often people want to talk about exploring their career and end up talking to anyone who will listen. This is important, but it's also imperative to know who to talk to and when, and to make sure you stagger your conversations by talking to the least professionally-relevant people while you are brainstorming and figuring out what you want to say. Save the most relevant professional contacts until you are clear as to what you want and you have your elevator pitch nailed down. For instance, you probably will only get one shot with a senior person at an organization, so don't schedule it until you are ready for 'that' conversation.

For example, if you are first brainstorming a career change, talk with your family or your friends about it; don't have that conversation with someone you might want to work for or a key person within the sustainability network. Save that conversation for once you've figured out exactly what you want to do.

This happens all the time. People come to me, or one of the Masters listed in this book, because someone told them that we know many people in the industry. The reality is that they will likely only get one meeting with us - ever. Therefore, if they come to us during the 'figuring it out stage,' they've just blown an opportunity to connect with us later on when they have a better grasp as to what they are looking for.

2. Prepare for the person you're meeting with

Preparation is essential. First of all, let the person know why you are meeting with them. Then, make sure to not only know their business inside and out, but the person you're meeting with as well.

Whether you're networking online or in person, it's imperative that you research and get to know people ahead of time. Google them and look up their LinkedIn profile and take notes. Know as much about the person as you can - where they went to school, their current role, their job history, etc.

You'll want to approach every networking opportunity thoughtfully because you'll be better equipped to find conversation topics, think of questions and discover things that you have in common (hobbies, interests, where they're from, networking groups they belong to or something as simple as that they've traveled to places you've both traveled to).

By being prepared, something may come up in your conversation that will help you. On the flip side, if you ask them something that is readily available online (Google, website, LinkedIn profile) this will tell them that you are unprepared and that you are wasting their time because you didn't even look them up.

- It's imperative you don't just show up to a coffee with someone and say, "Tell me about your job and what you did prior to this position"

- You'll want to dig deeper in your meeting, not just touch on the superficial stuff. Know the answers to the traditional 'get to know you' questions before you arrive so that you can use your time efficiently, effectively, and to talk about what you need to do

Beyond researching the person and the company, make sure you do the legwork on what you're looking for in a position. Don't count on that from the person you are interviewing with. There is nothing more annoying than for someone to say, "I'm looking for a job in sustainability and wanted to know what companies you think I should look at?"

Come to the meeting with a list of companies and contacts of places you've already looked at and places you are dismissing and why. You want the person you are meeting with to be able to help open doors and give contacts. So rather than saying, "Who should I talk to?" You'll want to come having looked at the 20 firms in your region and then have three to five that you want to know more about.

Come in with at least four questions prepared ahead of time. This is important in case you get nervous. Plus, if they ask you if you have any questions, you'll be prepared.

3. Be clear as to what you are looking to accomplish
Not everyone you talk with or ask to coffee is for the same reason. So have your elevator pitch down for what you want to do, but also tailor the reason as to why you are talking to someone based on what you are looking to accomplish from that specific conversation.

For example:
- If you need help figuring out what to do with your life, then have that conversation
- If you just want to get to know some people in a given industry, give them some examples of industries and companies that you are interested in ahead of time so that they can have responses ready
- If you're trying to meet with someone who's going to connect you with somebody else, make it clear and concise as to who you want to connect with

- If you are just looking to find some contacts in your desired industry, then come with a few names of people you are hoping to meet
- If you want to meet with someone about a potential job at their company, then have that elevator pitch down

> *"Practice your pitch, elevator speech and even interview questions - even film it on your phone if you can't stand listening to your own voice without a meltdown!"*
> Claudia Capitini—Founder and Principal, Maven Consulting, LLC[xxii]

4. Be respectful of the person's time

Realize that people are busy so don't ask if you can meet with someone this week, ask for it to be at least a few weeks out. If you ask for 20-30 minutes, keep it to that time and be very specific about what you want to accomplish, then target your conversation. You should always budget more time in case the meeting goes long, but assume the other person may have a meeting right afterwards. One hint: ask for coffee, not lunch. Multiple lunches will get expensive quickly, and if you find that you don't have a lot to talk about, then you are stuck there for an hour.

5. Consider what you can do for them

A huge mistake most job searchers make is to be so concentrated on their own job search that they fail to think about "What's in it for the person I'm meeting with?" or "How can I be of value to them?"

- Come prepared with some specific ideas. For example, "I understand you have lots of clients in 'X' field, and I tend to bump into these sorts of people at networking events. Would it beneficial if your products/services came up in conversation that I refer them to you?"

- Make sure you don't wait until the end to ask, "So how can I help you?" If you wait until the end, the person may just want to leave and not give you anything to reconnect with them about. Plus, you'll put yourself more on an equal standing if there is back and forth during the conversation

- Do NOT offer to volunteer to help them in some way unless you have thought this through and are committed to delivering. It may seem

like a good thing to do, but this person has never worked with you
before and knows nothing of your skills and work ethic. If there is
something specific (research, for example) and you'd be willing to do
it for free, then offer that up, but for the most part, don't offer unless
you are committed to delivering a solid work product

- Stay in touch; find articles/stories that are relevant to keep in
contact. While doing so, update them on your progress, and remind
them of your interest and ideas. There is nothing that ticks off
someone more than for them to give you their time and then to
never hear from you again. Remember, if you keep in touch, you may
be able to call on them when an opportunity presents itself

- Never assume your email is confidential. Odds are that about 90% of
the time, they'll forward your email to someone, so make sure it is
clean - especially if it was part of an email chain at some point

6. Make meaningful introductions
If you can introduce the person you are meeting with to someone they'd like
to get to know, they'll value you more because you've helped them out. So
look for ways to make meaningful introductions. For example, if they ask
you to make an introduction for them, do it! Call that desired contact and ask
them if you can connect the two. Then once they say it is okay, make an e-
introduction and then follow up with both contacts. If you just connect
people without alerting the desired contact, they may not know the context
and gloss over it and forget about it within a few hours.

7. Value your network
LinkedIn isn't Facebook. You need to be able to vouch for people in your
network. Only accept people to your LinkedIn network and refer people that
you can vouch for.

8. The importance of proper etiquette

Regardless of your connection or relationship with the person you're networking with, realize that etiquette is your ultimate business card.

No matter your skill level, no matter your age or position, there is no reason for not displaying proper etiquette. If you are unsure as to how to act in a certain situation, always err on the side of being over-polite, over-dressed, more respectful and deferential to age and experience.

For example:
- If you're in Gen X, you need to approach baby boomers with a different level of etiquette than how you would approach a millennial due to the different social norms
- If you're a millennial and you're used to talking with people in a very casual way, realize that when you meet with people who are a little older or are of a different generation, their expectations of etiquette are going to be different. Meet people at their level of etiquette, not yours

This means:
- Do not be overly casual, good etiquette may be forgotten, but if you display poor etiquette, they will remember it for years (see case study below)
- Honor confidentiality
- Know the expectation of the other side. For older generations, it is customary to first get to know the other person – where they are from, where they went to school, etc. Whereas in the tech industry, some companies want to dispatch with that and just get down to business right away
- Realize that if you ask for a coffee or lunch meeting, then you are buying
- Remember they are people too. They may not remember your name or what you do. When you reach out and shake their hand, state your name. This will alleviate awkwardness on their side if they have indeed met you before and forgotten your name or how you met.
- Follow-through with any commitments or comments you make

Case Study on Respect:
People may not remember your name or what you do, but if you have poor etiquette, that will end up being the only thing they remember about you, and potentially forever.

Three years ago I was speaking at the Go Green Conference in Seattle. Some of my former students were chatting in a small group so I walked over to talk to them. There were also several other people in the group that I didn't recognize so I introduced myself. One individual reached out and said, "Yeah, we've met before." I couldn't place it, so I replied, "I'm sorry, what is your name again?" She told me her name, but then said, "I actually met you two years ago, and you never remember my name!"

Now I'm someone who is actually pretty good with names, but I've also given about 300 talks in the last few years and on average, I meet over 1,000 new people each year. I was trying to kindly acknowledge that I didn't know her name and asked for it again, but because she responded they way she did, all I thought to myself was, "Well, now that I know her name, I can be darn sure I'll never recommend her to anyone, ever!"

Networking Reminders

- If you are trying to connect with someone, call or write, don't email. Busy Executives get close to 200 emails a day, but maybe two to four letters via mail, and probably only between 10-20 calls per day. Your chances are much better if you opt for an option other than email. Take a risk and differentiate yourself

- Always have business cards and a pen in your pocket to take notes after you have conversations with people

- If you are attending an event. Scan the name tags of the other attendees when signing in. Pick three or four people that you would like to meet. You can ask people you know or the host at the registration table to potentially introduce you

- When having conversations, first seek to understand, then to be understood. Ask where a person is from. You are more likely to find a personal connection than a professional one and it will open up the flow of conversation. Then ask what they do in their job. In return, they will likely ask you about your job

- From all of this, you can subtly drop in, "Well, if you ever want to talk about a carbon footprint (or whatever you may have been talking about), I'd be happy to grab a cup of coffee with you or pop by your office for 30-45 minutes to discuss this further with you"

- Remember to be an active listener. Think about whom else you may be able to connect this person to. If it is obvious to you that the person you are talking to is not a fit for your type of work, then think of your network and who it might be beneficial for you to connect them to. This increases your value as a connector

Tips for Networking at Events

Use listening to your advantage

Be present and listen. A lot of times extroverts spend all of their time telling people who they are but miss the important 50% of listening and learning about the other person. Be polite, spend quality time with each individual you're talking to, and never do what I call the 'New York Overlook,' meaning that you are listening while looking over the shoulder of the person you are talking to.

Embrace the uncomfortable person

I often tell colleagues to find someone who is alone and looks uncomfortable or maybe even nervous. We've all been in that role before and there's obviously a reason that person is uncomfortable. Just go introduce yourself to them, ask them their name and find out a little bit about them. This will take all of that pressure off of you. Plus, they might be thinking, "I like this person, you've made me feel good about myself and have helped me, I want to return the favor."

Volunteer at events and conferences

If you are a student or don't have a lot of money, see if you can volunteer and help out at registration. This may give you a discounted entry fee, but more importantly the ability to meet all of the attendees as they walk in the door. When you are checking people in, be sure to engage them by saying, "Welcome, I'm Samantha and I'm really looking forward to your presentation later." This is also a great way to meet people without having to walk up to them individually. Two more tips about conferences:

- Make sure you go to breakout sessions as they tend to be smaller and more intimate
- If you find yourself cancelling on attending events because it's nice out or you just don't feel up to it, sign up for events that cost money (you'll be less likely to cancel on events that you paid money for)

Set meetings up before the event/conference

Due diligence also applies to events and conferences because the best way to meet the person you want to talk to is to seek them out ahead of time. If you sign up for a large conference, see if there's an attendee list you can get from the organizer. If there is, reach out to the people you want to connect with and let them know that you'll be there and set up a meeting, coffee or lunch ahead of time.

Of course, in an ideal world, you'll have time to connect with everyone you want to at a conference, but the reality is that there's very limited time between sessions and it can be very difficult to connect with people on the fly. For example, if I go to a conference with 300 people, I might have only three people that email me ahead of time but in the back of my head I know I should be looking for them because they wanted to connect. By them reaching out and saying, "Hey, can we connect during the Tuesday A.M. coffee break," they've already set up a meeting or a connection that wasn't there.

Using technology at events
When you're at an event, use the Banjo app to let you know who's going to be attending and who's already in the room based on your LinkedIn, Twitter, Facebook and Instagram accounts. That way if you are at a large event and if you are wondering if someone you know or want to meet is there, social media can help you find them, and even help you set a meeting time or place.

Don't collect and pass out every business card
Once you get to the point where you're starting to pass out business cards, whether it's the shy person or someone you just had a conversation with, only pass out your card when it seems appropriate and after you've had a quality interaction. Don't just go up to somebody and leave your card because they don't know anything about you - who wants a card from someone they don't know at all? If you've had a good conversation, be sure to ask for theirs as well. If they don't have one, offer your card and have them write their contact information on the back of it. This may seem needy, but remember the important thing is for you to have their contact information and to follow up with them.

The importance of following up
I tell people that the follow-up is just as important as the connection. There is no point in going to an event and getting a bunch of cards, making a number of connections and then not following up. So when you're at an event, after every four or five people, be sure to find a place to write on the back of each card a few things to remind you about the conversation that you had with that person. Write down points to follow up on, whether it is professionally or if there is something you personally have in common (school, hobby, sports team or whatever it is you talked about). Having those notes will be helpful for re-connecting in the future and they will have an easier time remembering you, too!

The Differences Between Introverts and Extroverts

As you approach networking, it's important to understand the difference between introverts and extroverts, and that they approach things differently. Extroverts:

- Tend to jump into social situations without a lot of guidance
- Are comfortable talking and thinking on the fly
- Enjoy socializing and conversing in larger groups
- Gain energy from conversation and sometimes facilitating conversation
- Think that everyone is like them

The reality is that not everyone's personality is set up the same way. Extroverts have just as many challenges as introverts do. Extroverts might have an advantage in that they gain energy from talking to people and are often more willing to start a conversation. But they might talk so much that the listener can't remember their elevator pitch. And they can run around and talk to so many people that at the end of the day they can't remember who they talked to about what.

Introverts, however, are the exact opposite, they:
- Prefer to listen
- Like to watch and reflect on what's going on before speaking
- Are a little more risk-averse and hesitant to walk right up to someone and start talking - especially if there's a group of people
- Prefer to network in small groups and in one-on-one situations rather than in large groups
- Choose to observe others talking first before they do because they tend to have this bank of energy which diminishes over time, so the more that they're talking the more their energy goes down (introverts generate ideas and energy from internal sources, such as personal reflection)

Everyone has strengths and weaknesses, and there's definitely a perception that extroverts have an incredible advantage in networking, but that isn't necessarily true, it's just a different skill set. Introverts can be amazing networkers too, they just have to understand their skills and how to best deploy their skills in certain situations. Be sure to understand yourself and get to the core of whether you are introverted or extroverted as this may help you play to your strengths.

Key points for introverts if you are networking in person:
1. Get comfortable with your elevator pitch before you get there - know exactly who you are and what you want to say so that when you get there you're not nervous. Extroverts are happy to 'just wing it.'

2. Prepare some questions and conversation starters ahead of time such as, "Where are you from? How long have you been in this position? Tell me about some of the challenges your company is facing." Or bring up something about your local sports team or current events, but avoid religion and politics.

3. Get there early. As people trickle in, you'll have a better chance to get people one-on-one. If you show up and there are already 100 people in the room it can be overwhelming.

4. If you're scared to walk into a room by yourself, bring a friend or a colleague with you because you can use that person as a sounding board. It's also sometimes a lot easier breaking into conversations as a two-person team than it is as a single person.

   For example, we've all been to events where there are small circles of people standing and talking. Sometimes it can be really hard to break into one of these groups as an individual. Therefore, by working as a team you can introduce your friend to the person you want to meet, let your friend do the talking and start the conversation. That way, when the conversation comes back around to you, you'll have had a chance to listen to the conversations and determine how best to insert yourself.

5. Make a checklist ahead of time about what you want to accomplish and who you want to meet at an event. Think about why you are there. Are you there to see a particular speaker, to meet someone specifically, or just to come away with five or six new connections in your industry? That way, when your energy level starts to diminish, you can reflect on your checklist and what you went there to do. This will remind you to focus on who you came to talk to and why.

6. When networking, don't be afraid to recharge. If you've been doing a bunch of talking and your energy level is drained, go find a quiet place: check your phone, grab some water or some food and find a way to recharge your battery. But if your energy is 100% gone, and you know you have nothing left, then that's okay. It is time to leave and head home.

7. Ditch the lingo. Be professional and remember that whatever lingo you used at your school or in your office, people you've just met will not understand.

Online Networking - Social Media

For many, it may seem like online networking is easier because you are so familiar with social media. I'm going to provide high-level suggestions and then go into details about the different nuances for each type of online networking site.

If you're trying to figure out which industry leaders to follow and connect with, then hop on LinkedIn and Twitter and highlight hashtags about the industries and/or companies you are interested in. Join groups and start following industry conversations and you will begin to start recognizing who are the experts in your field.

You may find yourself thinking that you need a direct link with the person you're trying to connect with, meaning that you can only network to that person, A to B. The reality is that more often than not you are only one or two connection points away from the person. That's why LinkedIn is so important because you can mine your network, as well as your connections, to find a bridge (a person who can connect you with your desired contact) as opposed to always looking directly from A to B.

Instead of just using your current social network, make a concerted effort professionally to follow the people, companies, and thought leaders in your industry, and look for ways to connect with them online. Simply by liking their posts, commenting and even writing professional posts of your own on the subjects you are interested in will boost your ability to network with them.

LinkedIn

For professional purposes, LinkedIn is your most critical platform. People are expected to vouch for one another and it is a place to ask colleagues for referrals. So make sure you spend time on LinkedIn and have an updated and easy-to-understand resume, as well as a professional photo.

Keep your professional network tight and avoid accepting everyone who offers you an invite, as you'll want to be able to vouch for people and the quality of their work. I would say that about 50% of the time you have great connections and 50% time you'll find yourself screening against those people that you don't know.

In addition, make your profile look as professional and forward looking as possible - it should be formatted for the job you want, not the job you have! Use your LinkedIn profile to talk about who you are and what you want to be, not just what you've done. Also, when you receive the daily report of who has checked out your profile, go ahead and check them out, too, because they had a reason to look at you. If they are someone you recognize as a thought leader or are in your industry, use this opportunity to connect with them and send a message.

Twitter

Twitter is a great way to build your network. You can follow topics that are of interest to you, find job postings and follow both news and influencers in your industry. Click to follow companies and individuals you are interested in. Connect with industry influencers by re-tweeting and interacting with them on subjects that are important to you. While this may not lead directly to a networking opportunity, when you meet these people you will have conversation topics and they may even recognize you from your activity on social media.

Google Alerts

Another way to strengthen your online networking is to set Google Alerts on the subjects you care about and the companies and industries you're interested in. Google Alerts send a digest of these subjects to your inbox every single day. This will help you stay up to date and can provide you with talking points or information that you otherwise might not have seen in your normal day to day. If you are active on Twitter, Facebook or LinkedIn but don't have enough to say, having Google Alerts can help provide you with content to add to the conversation.

Warning About Social Media

Realize that anything you post to the general public on Facebook or Twitter *will* be seen by recruiters. In fact, according to the social media career site Jobvite, in its 2015 Recruiter Nation Survey, "Only 4% of recruiters DON'T use social media in the recruiting process." [xxiii] Be diligent about what you have online and delete or un-tag anything that you wouldn't want to one day show up on your boss' or future employer's screen.

Worksheet 6: Mapping Your Connectors

(Adapted from Elyn Andersson's Social Network Mapping work)

We all have friends, family and co-workers. These are people that we call our network. Depending on your personality, you may have a small network, or if you are active on Facebook, Instagram, or Pinterest, you might already have a large network. Even if you don't use any of these online platforms, chances are that you generally know people within your social circles that are connected. This exercise will help you identify who are the "connectors" in your own network. These are the people you most need to connect with both for your job search and to grow your network.

Instructions:
Read each category. Think of your top four people in each category and then rank them.

SOCIAL INSIDER = A friend who shares a large number of friends with you. Who are your top four social insiders? They can help you approach mutual friends in a less direct manner than if you reach out to people directly.

    1._____

    2._____

    3._____

    4._____

SOCIAL OUTSIDER = A friend who shares, at most, one mutual friend. Who are four of your social outsiders? These are people who, if you connected with better, could potentially expand your network because you know different groups of people.

    1._____

    2._____

    3._____

    4._____

SOCIAL CONNECTOR = A friend who connects groups of your friends together that otherwise would not.

Who are four of your social connectors? These are valuable people because they open up a larger group of people all at once.

1._____

2._____

3._____

4._____

MAVENS = A friend with a large number of out-of-network friends (they have a lot of other friends that you don't know) is called a maven. This is the group you want to focus on because they know you AND they know a bunch of people you don't know.

Who are four Mavens from your network?

1._____

2._____

3._____

4._____

If you haven't spoken directly with any of these mavens recently, send them a private message asking how they are, or invite them out for coffee!

The Importance of Seven Touches

This is a philosophy that I've learned and embraced throughout my professional career. The idea is that it takes about seven touches with someone before they begin to view you as a part of their network. So when you're thinking, "How do I connect with that CSR Director?" Don't just think about it as a one-off connection, conversation, or coffee, but think of it as a first step to them accepting you into their network. You likely won't register on their radar after just one, two or even three touches, so that's why the fourth, fifth, sixth, and seventh connection is so important.

How do you do this? Use the following example:

Let's say I want to meet the CSR manager of eBay so I look through my LinkedIn account until I find someone who knows that person. My first step is to send my contact a personal message to see if they'll connect me with the CSR Director at eBay.

Touch #1: My contact makes an e-introduction over LinkedIn and suggests that the two of us meet in person.

Touch #2: I send a personal message to that CSR manager and offer to buy them coffee.

Touch #3: When the person responds, I set up a time for a meeting.

Touch #4: While preparing for our meeting, I remember an article that is applicable to our conversation so I forward that along.

Touch #5: We meet in person over coffee.

Touch #6: Afterwards, I send her a handwritten note.

I know that sounds super cheesy and especially if you're younger, you're thinking, "Who sends hand written notes by mail?" That's the point. Hardly any of us get mail anymore – we get tons of emails and texts, but we never get mail. By taking the time to communicate how much their time meant to you, you will stick out and have differentiated yourself.

Okay, you now have *six* connections with this CSR Manager. The next crucial step is to take action on whatever advice they gave you in your meeting and then let them know that you did so. Remember to do this whether it's within a few days or two months out. This is your seventh connection. Eventually you'll run into them again, either in person or online, but now you will have built a rapport and you will have gained their acceptance. More often than not at this point, they'll respond with something as simple as, "Glad I could help" or, "Let me know if I can help you again at some point."

You have turned your 'contact' into someone in your network in seven touches!

Worksheet 7: The Seven Touches Worksheet

Instructions:
This exercise will help you map out how you could potentially meet up with or connect with your identified connection by using my Seven Touches framework.

1. First identify the three people you most want to network with. Who are your targets?
2. Then map out a potential strategy for bringing them into your network or making that important connection with them in seven touches.
   Tip: This could be through coffee, referrals, LinkedIn, social media, connection from a friend, social gathering, networking event, conference, etc. It's up to you.

Target 1: _____

Target 2: _____

Target 3: _____

Building Your Network

Develop a system that won't let you slack off

Networking is hard, so putting a system in place will help give you the discipline you need to avoid feeling like you're too busy or finding other things to do instead. Set aside a specific time and put it on your calendar (even if you have a job) to do your research, outreach, make follow up calls and emails. If you are currently in a job search or are a student then you need to spend even more time on this. For someone currently looking for work, this means at least an hour per day or five hours per week. For a graduating student, it is closer to 5-15 hours a week. I realize that it is so easy to get caught up in the day to day, especially in your senior year or final year of graduate school - but you need to build this into your calendar just like it's an important team meeting, paper, or test you need to prepare for.

"Persevere. There is perhaps nothing worse on the planet than job searching. Transitioning can be one rough ride, but stick to it! One of my running coaches once said to me while marathon training, "the pain of discipline is not nearly as bad as the pain of regret or a job poorly (or painfully, in that case) done." I think this applies to mid career job switches as well as pretty much anything in life." Claudia Capitini—Founder and Principal, Maven Consulting, LLC[xxiv]

Know your flow

Build this time into your day when it is out of your flow, meaning when you are the least productive or you lose concentration at work. If you're someone that likes to get to work and is really productive from 8am to 2pm and you start losing steam after 2pm, set time on your calendar from 2-3pm to send emails, network, or grab that coffee with potential contacts because you'll be unproductive in the office during these times anyways. Find the time that is best for you and put in a system to help you stay disciplined and stick to it.

If you already have a job and you feel like you're really rocking it, the reality is that you still need to network because you may need to find people within your organization that can help you solve a certain challenge, or that you will need to know to rise up the career ladder.

Lastly, networks take time and you need to build yours *before* you need it. It is easy to get caught up in our day-to-day lives, but you don't want to get caught flat-footed if your boss leaves and the replacement stinks, or your company does a round of lay-offs. Always be building your network whether you've got a job or not, because it takes time and you are always going to need it.

Multiply your contacts

Building your network isn't about how many people you know, it's about who you know and how to get introduced to the people *you need to know*. How do you do this? By multiplying and leveraging your contacts! Let's say, for example, that you start with a list of 10 people. By meeting these 10 people and asking each of them for two or three additional people for you talk to, all of a sudden you have now multiplied your network to 30 people. Then if you can get two connections from each of those people, you've now gone from your original 10 people to 60 people in no time.

If you want to be an effective networker, expand your horizons. Remember to do your due diligence, understand the differences between introverts and extroverts and use the power of seven touches and multiply your contacts. Networking is a skill, not a personality trait, but it requires practice, discipline and constant attention. Get started on it today!

Where Do I Look for Jobs in This Field?

If you're asking yourself, "Where do I start looking?" There are a number of great job sites in the field of sustainability, way more than I can list, but below are some that I turn to when referring job seekers.

Disclaimer: The links to these sites and their URL's are subject to change, so if they don't work at the time you search for them, simply Google the site. Spend some time and build your own.

URL Links
- www.sustainablebusiness.com
- www.greenbiz.com
- www.ecojobs.com
- www.ejobs.org/states/mi.html
- www.eco.org
- www.bsr.org
- www.jobmonkey.com/main/index.html
- www.environmental-expert.com/jobs.asp
- http://www.nature.org/about-us/careers/index.htm
- www.environmental-jobs.com
- www.sustainablebusiness.com
- http://www.greenjobs.net/
- http://www.ecoemploy.com/
- https://ecotrust.org/join-us/#jobs
- www.greenempowerment.org
- www.groundspring.org
- https://www.sustainabilityprofessionals.org/resources/career-resource

In addition to job sites, it is important to browse member-based organizations who might care about sustainability. For example, research if there is a Green Business Alliance or a sustainability committee at your local chamber. If so you'll find organizations that are interested in or are already working to integrate sustainability into their business. Look to see if there are any statewide or citywide trade organizations focused on sustainability or climate change in your area. Check out the member companies and contacts listed in the associations, go to their websites and find out how you can make a connection. For example, if you were in Seattle, WA, you'd want to create a list of organizations to check out like this:

- Green Drinks (seattlegreendrinks.org) – Free Networking and Drinks
- Network for Business Innovation and Sustainability (nbis.org) - Workshops and Events
- Net Impact Professional – Educational and Networking events
- Seattle Chamber of Commerce (seattlechamber.com) - Events and Networking
- Sustainable Seattle – Events and Workshops
- Greater Seattle Business Association – An alternative to the Chamber that is LGBTQ friendly
- Climate Solutions – Resources, events, ways to get involved on climate issues
- Washington Clean Tech Alliance (WCTA) – Monthly clean tech series
- Business Leaders for Climate Solutions – List of individuals in the sustainability space

Look in your city and region. Research and find organizations that have events and networking groups that you can attend, meet people and learn more about what is going on in this space locally.

"Start networking immediately - attend as many events as you can to get your name and face out to folks." Sean Schmidt—Office of Sustainability Assistant Director of Communications & Programs, University of Washington[xxv]

SECTION 6: INTERVIEWING AND INFORMATIONAL INTERVIEWS

Most of this section is focused on interviewing - how to prepare, questions to expect, how to put your best foot forward, and myths that need debunking.

Informational Interviews

Informational interviews are extremely important to your job search and you'll want to treat them just as professionally as you would a formal interview. You may not need to dress up fully, but it's important not to come off as nonchalant because it's 'only an informational interview.'

> *"Start networking early. It is never too early to start networking. Look for opportunities to conduct informational interviews - with visiting speakers in your classes, with other professionals at internships you have, with family friends who might do work you think you are interested in. But be sure to come prepared - do some research ahead of time and come with some key questions you want to ask." Jo Opdyke Wilhelm—Senior Ecologist, King County Waste and Land Resources Division[xxvi]*

The truth is, there is no such thing as an informational interview!

I state this quote often because every time I have given someone an 'informational' interview, I'm always wracking my brain to see if there is a way they can help my company or that of a friend's.

Realize that if you do set up a meeting with someone, come prepared because this might actually be 'THE' interview after all. I've hired people directly out of informational interviews or coffees simply because they impressed me and during our conversations I got to thinking that, "This person might just be perfect for this project."

However, if someone comes off poorly, then I do the complete opposite, I shut them out of my mind for a potential role (sometimes permanently) and when they ask for other people they should talk to or referrals, I usually don't give them out. So it's much more than just an 'informational.'

I write this because I remember when I was a senior in college and a friend of my parents got me an informational interview with American Express Financial Advisors. Although I dressed in a suit, I didn't come in prepared at all. I expected to simply have coffee, ask some questions and expected the gentleman to just show me the light. I didn't tailor my resume, have my elevator pitch down, or even think about what specifically I wanted other than a job in the financial services industry. Needless to say, I bombed. And I remember my parent's friend calling me and telling me how disappointed she was in me, because she had referred me to this person, and I had let her down too. Don't do that!

Therefore anytime you ask for someone's time, even if it is just for a simple cup of coffee or a drink after work, take it seriously because you may actually be getting screened just like you would for an interview. Come prepared, dress appropriately and bring a copy of your resume in case they ask for it. Of course, make sure to have pen and paper ready to take notes and write down any advice or leads they may give you.

Keeping track of your informational interviews

Below is an example of a way to keep track of your coffee dates and informational interviews.

Name	Company	Email	When did I meet them?	Points to remember	Follow- Up
Brent Rivard	Corporate Cleaners	BrentR@cclean.com	Annual Eco Products Conference	Has client looking for green cleaning/product options	Set up a date for coffee in next two weeks
Anna Turnquist	Anna's Weddings	AnnaT@wedrus.com	Green Drinks 9/15	Looking for ways to 'green' weddings and is looking for a consultant to help her	Refer her to Amy's friend Jenny who just did that for her wedding
Dan McKane	Morgan Stanley	DMckane@ms.com	Chamber After Hours 9/1	Broker - was asked by a friend about SRI investing. Looking for tips	Send link to article on SRI figures

Interview Checklist and Prep

The more relaxed and prepared you are, the better you will do in an interview. Before you step into an interview, remember these key steps: go in confident and have your story, skills, and ideas dialed in. This checklist will help you before, during and after.

A. The week before the interview

Preparation can beat skills! Find out everything about the company, its sustainability actions (on its website, CSR report, social media) and research the interviewers if you can. Follow what was mentioned in the prior networking section, get to know everything about the company and them from their profiles on LinkedIn or company website. If you can find a common connection early on, and they begin to like you, they will be more likely to help you during the interview. Also, if there is a professional accomplishment that's worth mentioning, for example, they wrote a book or an article you've read, be sure to highlight that. But be authentic, if you haven't read the book then make sure you at least skim it.

- Take out a sheet of paper and on the left side write down all of the requirements and skills in the job description. Then on the right side, match your experiences or ability to handle each of these, so that you have responses ready. Highlight specific examples from your work and successes. For example, "Yes, at company 'X' I did 'Y' and our team was able to reduce our carbon footprint by 20% in two years by doing these things."

- Anticipate their needs and how you can meet them. Compare the needs in the job description to what you've read about the company and try to both anticipate what their needs are, why, and have a few answers as to how you can help solve these problems. Remember, if you think they are looking for 'X,' make sure you have the answer ready for 'X' and don't start a response by telling them all that you can do about 'W,' 'Y,' and 'Z.'

"First, I look for whether they truly understand the challenges and opportunity that my organization is facing." Dan Stonington—Executive Director, NW Natural Resource Group[xxvii]

For example, if one of the main responsibilities is to manage the company's social media, then research their entire social media platform, read through it, and find out if there was someone in the role before you (maybe there wasn't). Then come up with specific instances where you've helped an organization achieve results similar to what this company is looking for. Be the solution to their problem.

"Think about how to leverage past experience into a role that incorporates sustainability. Sustainability involves project management, cross-functional team leadership, communication, and so much more. Chances are much of the work you've done plays into this." Sarah Martinez—Sustainability Maven, Eco Product[xxviii]

- Have your story nailed and be concise, about one to two minutes. Why are you here? What led you to this job? And then tie it to the job you're applying for and why you are excited to work there.

- Be prepared for behavioral or problem solving questions, such as "How do you handle ambiguity?" "Tell me about a time where you had to work with a difficult co-worker." "Tell me about your worst experience at a job." "Tell me about your best team experience and why this was the case." "Tell me about a time when you had to turn a failure into a success." Employers want to understand how you'll handle situations, not just your skills.

- Have your list of questions for them ready. Make it a two way conversation within at least the first 20 minutes. The more conversational, the better, so have questions ready for them about the job and company beyond anything that can easily be found on the website. When someone asks me, "So who are some of the clients you've worked with?" We list those right on our website, and that immediately shows me that they didn't prepare.

- Determine your salary needs ahead of time. Have three scenarios. First think through what the base salary will be based upon what is listed in the description. Then create a 'best case' as to what you'd like to earn and ask for, and also have a 'worst case,' meaning this is the absolute lowest you can go on salary and benefits.

- If possible, ask a reference or two (if they may know someone within the company or the person you are interviewing with) to reach out and drop an email or call *before* your interview. This is a great way to provide 'street cred' about you and may help grease the skids before you go in.

B. Questions to expect

1. Tell us a little bit about yourself.
2. Why are you interested in this job? (Remember, people want to hire people who want this specific job, not just any job)
3. If sustainability related – what first got you interested in this field? Why?
4. How much do you know about our company and our culture?
5. What is your greatest strength? Then be prepared to answer – What is your greatest weakness?
6. Tell us about your greatest professional achievement? Where was this?
7. How do you handle conflict? With co-workers? With a boss?
8. Can you provide us with an example of your leadership skills?
9. Give us an example of a time you worked with a highly functioning team? What role did you play?
10. What do you do if a co-worker's performance is not up to par? How will you handle this?
11. Why do you believe you are the best candidate for this position?
12. Describe your ideal work environment. Do you work best alone and quietly, or in a fast-paced, louder environment?
13. What stresses you out? How do you handle pressure?
14. What are your long term goals? And how does this job play into that? Is this a stepping stone or end destination?
15. What do you do outside of work? What do you do for fun?
16. Travel may be part of this job, will that be a problem?
17. Are you willing to relocate?
18. How much do you want to earn?

C. Before you go to the interview

Remember that professional appearance matters. Even if you already know the person, always dress for success. If you are unsure of the attire, always err on the side of over dressed versus under because and you can always remove a scarf or take off a jacket and tie if need be. But you'll never be able to add on. If you can, ask someone inside the company or look at photos of employees on the company's website. If people are pictured in jeans and t-shirts, then dress business casual, but if they are in suits, then you need to look your very best! Borrow some clothes from a buddy if you have to!

- Make sure you have the address and map it out with printed directions in case your phone dies
- Have the telephone number of the headquarters or the receptionist of the person you are interviewing in case of emergency
- Leave 20-30 minutes more time than you think you need in case there is traffic
- Dress to impress, go to the bathroom and check yourself in the mirror to make sure you have nothing in your teeth and that your collar is up right. Some of your confidence will come from feeling and looking good
- Get your energy level up by stretching in the bathroom or doing jumping jacks to get your blood flowing. Your initial impression will be the lasting one, so arrive with positive energy

D. *Carry these items to the interview*

- Extra copies of your resume and have two more than you think you'll need
- A pad of paper to take notes. If you don't have anything, it may convey that you aren't taking the interview seriously. Plus, they may say something that you'll need to remember for a second round interview
- A copy of your references
- It goes without saying, but turn OFF your cell phone

E. *Upon arrival*

- Arrive early but not too early. You can arrive in the building early, but don't show up for the interview more than five minutes early. Grab coffee if you arrive too early. Oftentimes the interviewers need time to huddle before the meeting, so you'll want to honor/respect that
- Review your notes one last time before going in
- Greet your interviewer with a smile and offer a firm handshake, but don't crush their hand
- Maintain eye contact

"In an in-person interview I like to see that someone is confident and a self-starter without having an ego. As I tell many of the students I work with, you have to check your ego at the door every day when you work in sustainability."
Jeremy King— Campus Sustainability Coordinator, Denison University[xxix]

F. During the interview

- Relax and enjoy the conversation
- Find ways to weave into the conversation the points you want to make, without it sounding rehearsed
- Ask questions, listen and read between the lines. Don't wait too long to ask questions
- If you don't understand a question or are unsure of your answer, ask a clarifying question to give yourself more time to think of your response
- Don't bring up compensation unless they do. At the end, thank the interviewer, and ask about next steps
- Be sure to tell them you want the job and would be excited to work there. Most people think this is implied, but it often isn't. You never want them to think to themselves afterwards, "They were great, but I wasn't sure if they really wanted to work here or just land a job."

G. After the interview

- Go to a coffee shop or lunch spot and write down all of your notes, what you are thinking and feeling and the pros and cons. Interviewees often forget to say one or two important pieces of information during the interview. If that was you, make sure to weave them in when you send a follow-up thank you via email (within 24 hours)
- Write a thank you letter and get it in tomorrow's mail, don't wait a few days. Whatever you do, do not follow-up via text or IM, which just conveys too much casualness

Keeping track of jobs applied for

While you're busy with interviews and following the above steps, stay organized. Make sure you keep track of the process and the positions you have been applying for.

Company	Date	Position	Contact	Reply	Next Step
Starbucks	8/30	Barista, Green Team Lead	Matt Ides	No	TBD
REI	9/15	Associate	Matt Dietz	Yes	Call w/Mgr. in two weeks
Nature Conservancy	9/10	Office Mgr.	Mindy Clarke	Yes	2nd interview
Earth Share	9/2	Outreach Coordinator	Megan Kram	No	Hired someone else
Carbon Salon	8/22	Researcher	Elisabeth Terry	No	Hired someone else
Pappas PR	8/4	CSR Coordinator	Brett Rosenberg	Yes	Meet w/ green team

Three Interview Myths Debunked

Myth 1: The Interviewer is Always Prepared

The person interviewing you may have barely looked at your resume or they may just be someone sitting on a panel and have given no thought to your qualifications. You might be the first candidate they are talking to and they haven't really gotten their questions together yet. My advice - over prepare! Be ready to talk about yourself, explain your resume and think through what needs to be said.

Myth 2: The Right Questions Will be Asked

Sometimes interviews can go sideways and they start asking questions that don't let you really talk about your qualifications or get to the root of why you think you are the right person for the job. This often times happens in group interviews.

My advice - before you interview, be clear about the five things you want them to remember in case nothing else sticks. Find a way to answer a question by weaving these into your answers. Also make sure that you've definitely answered the following three things (in case they don't ask):

> a. Why do you want this job?
> b. How can you meet their specific need?
> c. Why are you the right person for their company and this role?

Myth 3: The Most Qualified Person Gets the Job

People want to find someone who can not only get the job done, but also fits their culture. Some of the other candidates may be more qualified than you, but maybe they aren't the correct fit for the company or department, or they have a personality that doesn't jive with the manager. Other candidates may be too qualified, in which case the company could be worried that they are going to be a 'know it all' or that they'll only be in the role for a few months and then jump ship because they might get bored.

My advice - Don't worry about the competition. Just be yourself. There is nobody that is more qualified to do that than you!

For example, if the job you are applying for feels like a reach based on 'years of industry experience,' then have a response that spins your inexperience into a positive trait. "I don't have the five years experience your job description asks for, but within my three years at company 'M,' I was able to do 'X, Y and Z'. And while not in your industry per se, I also have a year of experience doing what this job requires from my volunteer experience."

How to Acknowledge and Talk About Your Weaknesses

We all have weaknesses and are rarely the 'perfect candidate' for a job. Therefore, look at the job description and acknowledge to yourself what your weaknesses are or where you might have gaps when it comes to the job description. Then come up with how you are going to overcome these. For example, if someone asks you a question in an interview along the lines of, "Can you do X, Y, and Z?" Maybe you don't have 'Z,' but instead of discounting yourself, you can say, "No, I do not have 'Z,' but I have a strong network and I know people who do, whom I can call on and learn from before I start this role." This shows that you have the ability to solve problems and that you can utilize your network to not only make up for deficiencies, but show that you bring something bigger to the role than just yourself. Beyond using your network, you can also uncover experiences that you've had outside of the workplace and mine them for skills and techniques that you can communicate during an interview. The worksheet below will help you identify those experiences and transform them into qualifications.

Worksheet 8: Valuable Experience Outside of Work

All of us have life or personal experiences where we have excelled and many of these are applicable in a professional setting and can demonstrate you abilities to an interviewer.

These stories are meant to show you that despite your lack of experience in the workplace, you have had personal experiences where you've demonstrated the skills that employers are looking for and can pull from them during interviews to highlight your qualifications. Be sure to include skills and strengths you used to achieve each accomplishment.

Here are some examples that people have said to me during interviews where they've demonstrated the skills needed from their personal lives, since they hadn't had a chance to do so yet in a professional setting.

I haven't had to lead teams yet in a work setting, but in both high school and college, I was selected to be the captain twice, and was often looked to for leadership from the players, and served as a go-between from my coach to some of our younger players. I'm comfortable and excel in teams.	I had no formal teaching experience, but as a volunteer with the Boys and Girls Club, I was asked to teach young teens coping mechanisms for bullying and handling tough situations. Moreover, I was an upper middle class white kid teaching in a predominately socially and economically diverse community. Therefore, before I could teach the curriculum, first I had to gain their trust and confidence. I did this, and it was rewarding because many of the kids are still in contact with me today.
As a camp counselor at YMCA camp, I was often put in situations where I had to make quick decisions and improvise on the fly. I didn't have any EMT training, but we were on an outdoor trip and I was with one of the kids that was lagging behind. He ended up falling and having a major injury, but there was no cell service, no medical kit, and I had no formal training. However, I was able to calm him down, put pressure on the bleeding and we improvised a tourniquet until we hiked to the van and could get help.	When I was a sophomore in college I was asked to sing in my cousins wedding. I hadn't sung for years, so I was a bit nervous about this. However, I overcame this by listening to the song multiple times/day and then practicing two or three more times each day. On the day of the wedding, I got a 'surprise' and was told that I would be performing with my cousin who played acoustic guitar. This was a whole new style that I had not practiced for, and we only got a chance to run through it three quick times before the wedding. I ended up forgetting a line but the audience loved it and nobody noticed. I overcame my anxiety through discipline and practice, and was able to handle the switch to acoustics by being open to improvisation and highly prepared on my end.

In this worksheet, list six stories about a challenge and how you overcame it. Try to think of experiences where major skills were used (leadership, thinking on your feet, time management, discipline, learning on the job, working in teams, etc.).

1.	2.
3.	4.
5.	6.

BOOKS TO READ

Below is an incomplete list of books on Sustainability and Sustainable Business that I recommend for you to read. There are obviously other ones that I may have missed, but these are the essentials to get you going:

1. *The Sustainability Advantage* - Bob Willard
2. *Cradle to Cradle* - William McDonough and Michael Braungart
3. *Return on Sustainability* - Kevin Wilhelm
4. *Good to Great* - Jim Collins
5. *7 Habits of Highly Successful People* - Steven Covey
6. *Making Sustainability Stick* - Kevin Wilhelm
7. *What Matters Most* - Jeffrey Hollender
8. *The Fifth Discipline* - Peter Senge
9. *The Ecology of Commerce* - Paul Hawken
10. *Natural Capitalism* - Hunter Lovins
11. *The Way Out* - Hunter Lovins
12. *True to Yourself* - Mark Albion
13. *Let My People Go Surfing* - Yvon Chouinard
14. *Small Giants* - Bo Burlingham
15. *The Sustainability Handbook* - William Blackburn
16. *The Business Guide to Sustainability* - Darcy Hitchcock & Marsha Willard

TIPS FROM THE MASTERS

As I mentioned in the introduction, I didn't want this book to just be about what I've seen and experienced, but I wanted to share with you thoughts and suggestions from leaders in the field.

I call this section Tips From The Masters.

I asked these professionals with a combined 350 years of experience from the For-Profit, Non-Profit, Government, and Educational Sectors the following four questions. Their responses and quotes are incorporated throughout the book and bunched together below by category:

1. **What three bits of advice would you give an upcoming graduate trying to get a job in sustainability?**

2. **What are the two most important things that you look for in a candidate? Either on their resume or in-person?**

3. **If you had to tell a 30-40-year-old that is looking to do a career change, and wants to match their work with their values by getting into sustainability, what are the two most important things for them to know?**

4. **What is something that an aspiring sustainability professional should know, that nobody will tell them?**

What three bits of advice would you give an upcoming graduate trying to get a job in sustainability?

<u>Volunteer</u>

- Look for any opportunities to get experience and expand your network. Are there companies you really like or people you really like in those companies? Do some kind of work for them and/or with them. Take whatever they give you and then find your way to the sustainability people there. Take them out to coffee. *Derek Eisel— Director of Sales, Scope 5[xxx]*

- Get out there and get recognized! Attend networking events ... volunteering at a non-profit sustainability organization... volunteering at sustainability conferences (you can get in free this way) ... apply for an intern position (many companies accept interns their first summer after graduation). *Jackie Drumheller— Sustainability Manager, Alaska Airlines[xxxi]*

<u>CSR in Existing Job</u>

- My input to most folks about "CSR jobs" is – don't chase one. Use CSR skills to make you excel at your day job and get promoted faster. *Kevin Hagen, —CSR Director, Iron Mountain[xxxii]*

<u>First Seek to Understand</u>

- First thing, don't go into a company telling them what they need to do or should do. Instead learn (listen!) from them what they want to do and give them ideas on how to get this work done and why you have the expertise to do it. *Dan Moore—CEO, Pandion Consulting and Facilitation[xxxiii]*

Humility and Flexibility

- Secondly, present yourself with humility <u>and</u> passion! You need to have overflowing optimism while being ready to learn. *Dan Moore— CEO, Pandion Consulting and Facilitation*[xxxiv]

- Don't be above doing grunt work. The lessons you learn in the weeds are incredibly valuable in building a foundation of knowledge. *Sarah Martinez—Sustainability Maven, Eco Products*[xxxv]

- I think one of the keys to landing that first job is flexibility. If graduates are willing to move anywhere, work nontraditional hours, and take on unusual tasks out of the gate, it will pay off in the long run.
  Maggie Schilling—Administrative Director, Northern Rockies Conservation Cooperative[xxxvi]

- Be flexible. Sustainability roles, while more common than they used to be, are still really hard to find and now there are even more people competing for the same positions. Be geographically flexible. Consider taking an internship if it is a company you really want to work for. Be flexible in your time horizon to a sustainability role, meaning consider applying for conventional roles in a company you really admire. The role should still make use of your strengths and interests but can allow you to integrate sustainability elements into your role where appropriate and eventually transition to sustainability department. Your time in the business will give you deeper insights and more credibility and help forge relationships and will give you more options from a career path perspective. *Jake Swenson—Director of Sustainability, Staples*[xxxvii]

- Spend some time working in an organization doing "line" related work – in other words, learn the business in a role that is not necessarily in the sustainability department or role. *Cynthia Figge— Co-Founder and COO, CSR Hub*[xxxviii]

Perseverance

- And third, remember that turning the Titanic takes time. Don't give up if it doesn't happen overnight. *Dan Moore—CEO, Pandion Consulting and Facilitation[xxxix]*

- First and foremost, don't become disenchanted right away! Hold onto your sense of purpose as long as you can, just let it evolve and breathe as you go. Don't shrug and give up as the sometimes harsh realities of business shut down the fair share of your great ideas and projects. Simply doing something because "it's the right thing to do" frankly isn't going to happen. But that doesn't mean that all is lost; it just means that your sense of purpose must sharpen, focus, and weave its way into other channels like your written communications, public speaking, fiscal or budget planning, negotiation conversations.

  Never forget communication essentials like relationship building, emotional intelligence and negotiation skills either. These channels are the ways you can get your sustainability work done, and with a little breathing room, many of those great ideas do evolve into realistic projects on their own. *Claudia Capitini—Founder and Principal, Maven Consulting, LLC[xl]*

Apply CSR to Traditional Business Roles

- My first and most important suggestion is to emphasize the importance of understanding core, non-sustainable principles and widely accepted core practices whether it is accounting, finance, supply chain practices or whatever your underlying passion is.

  Sustainability is merely an extension of adapting these core skills to forming competitive business advantage through the adoption of broader cost savings (such as efficiency gains, reduction in waste or proactively adopting business practices to address changes in compliance standards such as carbon emission reductions), engaging a more broadly diversified universe of stakeholders (employees, communities and suppliers harmonized around a central goal) or product development aimed to serve newly forming markets. Sustainability by itself isn't a business but rather it is adoptive practice that enhances existing business and operating practices. *Patrick Drum— Portfolio Manager & Research Analyst, Saturna Capital[xli]*

- If you really want to drive change in a business, it's probably best to be in a core business function. You know who actually designs sustainable products? Product designers. You know who actually engages with suppliers on sustainable supply chain issues? Supply chain managers. So, it's important to think about what role you really want to play, and what best aligns with your skills and desires. *Sarah Martinez—Sustainability Maven, Eco Products[xlii]*

- Second, I would suggest mastering your basic skills in business, law, medicine, whatever it is so that you truly understand the space you want to work in. For example, if want to make skyscrapers as low impact and community friendly, you better have an understanding of real estate, law, city planning and finance as well as your sustainability knowledge. *Claudia Capitini—Founder and Principal, Maven Consulting, LLC[xliii]*

- Getting a job in sustainability is just like getting a job in any field. For instance, if you're coming from school, did you pursue a particular area of sustainability do your coursework? Did you do sustainability related work for a volunteer project organization outside of school? Did you do an internship during school? Even if the answer to all of these things is no, you probably still have a skill that can be applied in the field and sustainability. For example if you studied English, you can probably get a job doing marketing work, grant writing, or general communications for an organization If your training or interest is more technical (math or science) then it's likely you could find work doing analysis, economic or otherwise. In short, my advice is to pursue and hone your skills and your strengths, and then work to apply those by adding value of an organization involved in sustainability. *Eli Reich—Chief Alchemist, Alchemy Goods[xliv]*

- Don't be discouraged if you can't find a role with the word "Sustainability" in it – you can make huge impacts from anywhere you sit in an organization. *Janice Lichtenwaldt—Sr. Mgr IT Communications, T-Mobile[xlv]*

Reality check

- Don't try to be an expert in everything - you'll be wasting your time. *Jeremy King— Campus Sustainability Coordinator, Denison University[xlvi]*

- Be specific and credible about what you can actually do. If there is no clear story, be honest about being aspirational while doing your best to relate your goals to something you've succeeded at. *Jon Kroman— CEO, Kroman Law[xlvii]*

Language

- Sustainability is not a negative thing, don't let it or yourself get corrupted into something people dislike or even fear. Whether good or bad, any talk of sustainability makes the layperson nervous – finds ways to alleviate that. *Jeremy King— Campus Sustainability Coordinator, Denison University[xlviii]*

- Academia can sometimes give us a sense that the world 'outside the classroom' is aligned with the content that we've spent years studying. Like in any field, being out in the marketplace will offer you a wide array of viewpoints, understanding and awareness of sustainability issues. Knowing that you will not be speaking to one particular 'audience' and learning how to navigate different levels of awareness, concern and focus on sustainability can make you a more valuable team member and employee. *Molly Ray—Sr. Mgr Sustainability, Office Depot[xlix]*

Importance of Networking

- Network, network, network. Always ask if there is anyone else the person could connect you with, and always send an email afterwards, thanking them for their time. *Sarah Martinez— Sustainability Maven, Eco Products[l]*

- Even if it is not your favorite thing to do, work on your networking skills. For an employer, being able to put a face, a smile, and a friendly quick conversation behind a name on a resume puts that application miles ahead of the other candidates. *Maggie Schilling— Administrative Director, Northern Rockies Conservation Cooperative[li]*

- Join relevant networks and professional associations to build your contacts and learn what people in the field are doing. *Marsha Willard—CEO, Axis Performance Advisors[lii]*

Gain Experience/Intern

- Second, make sure to have some professional experience in the field in addition to a degree on your resume. Summer jobs or internships are invaluable in terms of demonstrating interest in and commitment to the field. *Maggie Schilling—Administrative Director, Northern Rockies Conservation Cooperative[liii]*

- Experience matters. It is important to get on the job experience through internships and summer jobs. This shows a commitment to pursuing a sustainability career path, helps separate you from other college students who may only have course work on their resume, and provides a valuable opportunity to network with other sustainability experts and helps you start figuring out what types of organizations and types of work you like and - just as valuable to learn - what don't like to do. *Jo Opdyke Wilhelm—Senior Ecologist, King County Waste and Land Resources Division[liv]*

- Build your resume; it is extremely important to seek internships as early as possible in your area of interest to develop stronger knowledge and skills regarding policies, processes, procedures, structure and research to build confidence about subject matter when later applying for a job. If an internship is not available and you can afford to, volunteer your time or discuss with your advisors to see if class credits can be provided for your time. Take the initiative and write to someone who inspires you for an internship opportunity! *Marianella Franklin— Chief Sustainability Officer, University of Texas-Rio Grande Valley[lv]*

- Sustainability jobs in companies are not very common, because it is an emerging field. Because of this, it is currently highly competitive to get into a role. Before you graduate, you need to have already started getting some experience and have begun to build a professional network. You can do this by: 1) volunteering or interning in an organization; 2) attending events and getting to know sustainability professionals in your region and 3) taking a role that doesn't have the title "sustainability" in it, and working to integrate the principles of sustainability into your day-to-day work to get experience. Go where you are needed -- this is probably in an organization that is just getting started in sustainability and needs an emerging leader to get it going. *Brenna Davis—Director of Sustainability, Virginia Mason/ Chair, WBCA[lvi]*

Stay Informed

- Finally, sustainability rock stars need to be able to speak to anyone and connect quickly. Read everything. For example, each day, I check in with nine online newspapers from around the world, cruise through a list of 30 of my favorite blogs, and listen to pod casts as I travel and in the car. That is of course in addition to my sustainability focused Twitter, Instagram, FB feeds. I follow everyone from the Supreme Court, leading fortune 500 companies to Jane Goodall, NASA, and even Bored Panda. Inspiration is everywhere. *Claudia Capitini—Founder and Principal, Maven Consulting, LLC[lvii]*

- Understand the players and business drivers for the industry. Who are the customers? How do they make buying decisions? What does the regulation landscape look like? How are they impacted by the company's sustainability efforts? *Matt O'Laughlin—Sustainability Manager, K2 Sports*[lviii]

- Make sure your base knowledge of sustainability and general sustainability implementation strategies is well oiled. *Marsha Willard—CEO, Axis Performance Advisors*[lix]

- Once you know what part of the field is right, get smart on it. If you want to work on corporate sustainability issues, there are dozens (if not hundreds) of news sources, blogs, organizations, conferences, etc. that you can track that will allow you to better understand the issues and players. This knowledge base will be invaluable as you network with people in the field and interview for positions. *Michael Sadowski—Director, Innovation Scale & Partnerships, Nike, Inc.* [lx]

Informational Interviews

- Setup informational interviews with companies, organizations, and agencies you want to work for with the same purpose...get your name and face out there. *Sean Schmidt—Office of Sustainability Assistant Director of Communications & Programs, University of Washington*[lxi]

Due Diligence

- Anticipate what each company needs when applying for open roles and position your strengths appropriately - Everyone loves a candidate who has done their homework and has a sense of the company and where the company is on sustainability journey. *Jake Swenson—Director of Sustainability, Staples*[lxii]

- Companies that are middle of the pack and don't have C-suite level support can still be doing good work, but maybe the culture hasn't really embraced sustainability. In those situations, you can't just have technical knowledge and passion; you need to be a change agent and internal consultant, with strong people skills to influence others. *Jake Swenson—Director of Sustainability, Staples*[lxiii]

- Other smaller companies may have C-suite support to start a sustainability program but have no idea what to focus on or what that means. Leadership companies may really want experts in a specific area that are part of larger team and it is more important that you know a specific issue area and have experience there versus other skills. *Jake Swenson—Director of Sustainability, Staples*[lxiv]

- Learn to think and work in an interdisciplinary manner. Offer concrete skills needed to get the job done. And lastly, think strategically, speak diplomatically, and act decisively. *Howard Sharfstein— Associate General Counsel – Environmental Sustainability, Kimberly Clark*[lxv]

- Do your homework on the organizations and people you engage. I generally enjoy giving informational interviews, particularly when the interviewer asks questions that show she knows my company, the issues we face and even my background. *Michael Sadowksi— Director, Innovation Scale & Partnerships, Nike, Inc.*[lxvi]

Know Yourself

- Sustainability is such a broad field and there is a tendency to think that we have to know everything about every aspect: waste, water, energy, procurement, etc. This can feel overwhelming when trying to find your place in this industry. Know what you do well...for example; are you a writer or creative type? Do you like spreadsheets and gathering data? Spend time figuring out your strengths and apply that to an aspect of sustainability. You will more likely perform better (and enjoy it more!) if it fits into existing skill sets and strengths. *Molly Ray—Sr. Mgr Sustainability, Office Depot*[lxvii]

- The field of "sustainability" is quite broad – corporate sustainability, consulting, responsible investing / finance, renewable energy, social enterprise, and so on. I would strongly suggest taking the time to consider what part of the field is most appealing and energizing, and where your skills can be best utilized. *Michael Sadowski—Director, Innovation Scale & Partnerships, Nike, Inc.*[lxviii]

Business Case

- Ensure you understand the underlying business case for sustainability, especially in your field of interest. Maintain your passion for the work but remember to make your case for sustainability with facts – passion without substance is not effective. *Janice Lichtenwaldt—Sr. Mgr IT Communications, T-Mobile*[lxix]

- Become as knowledgeable as possible about the environmental impacts and costs associated with those impacts of the product or service of the industry that you are interested in. *Matt O'Laughlin— Sustainability Manager, K2 Sports*[lxx]

Narrow Your Search

- Identify the sector and industries you would like to work in. Do you want to work in the nonprofit or for profit sector? Do you want to work in a large company or small, entrepreneurial company? Where do you want to work (urban, rural, virtual, office)? *Cynthia Figge— Co-Founder and COO, CSR Hub*[lxxi]

International Perspective

- Prove your passion; having a Global perspective of what is needed to achieve sustainable development is also very important. Search for study abroad programs/opportunities with a focus in sustainability initiatives. Participation on an international level can help build global perspective as well as build your resume! Write strong letters about your passion for sustainable development within your community and how a global perspective can help you bring innovation back home can also help you seek scholarship funding for your study abroad. *Marianella Franklin—Chief Sustainability Officer, University of Texas Rio-Grande Valley[lxxii]*

Niche

- Identify a niche to which you can contribute in the process and develop some specific expertise and/or experience in that niche. For example, it might be sustainability report, sustainability auditing, materials management, etc. *Marsha Willard—Co-Founder, International Society of Sustainability Professionals, ISSP[lxxiii]*

What's In It for Them?

- Ask yourself whether and how your capabilities in sustainability will promote the goals and values of the person you're speaking with, not yours. *Jon Kroman—CEO, Kroman Law[lxxiv]*

What are the two most important things that you look for in a candidate? Either on their resume or in-person?

Scrappy and Follow Instructions

- I look for people who are scrappy, who can start up a conversation with anyone, who do the work from their heart and who can follow instructions, but don't need them beyond some initial training. *Derek Eisel—Director of Sales, Scope 5*[lxxv]

- The specific skill set that I look for in a candidate greatly depends on the type of role they are interviewing for. Sales requires confidence, operations require rational thinking, etc, but beyond their skills, the most important overall characteristics are trustworthiness, grit and determination, positive attitude, and a strong ability to work constructively with others. *Eli Reich—Chief Alchemist, Alchemy Goods*[lxx]

- I look for determination and tenacity. Does this candidate seek difficult challenges? *Dan Stonington—Executive Director, NW Natural Resource Group*[lxxvii]

Facilitation

- I am intrigued when I see facilitation or community organizing on their resume. To be effective, a person needs to know how to listen and align their role with the objectives of the other people in the company. *Dan Moore—CEO, Pandion Consulting and Facilitation*[lxxviii]

<u>Language</u>

- Individuals in the sustainable community need to recognize that they are talking a different language to non-sustainable individuals. My experience isn't that these individuals don't support the notion of sustainability but rather just don't understand the context, expressed as what is the value enhancing proposition if were to employ sustainable practices. *Patrick Drum—Portfolio Manager & Research Analyst, Saturna Capital*[lxxix]

<u>Communication Skills</u>

- I want to see that the candidate has strong communications skills. This is probably the most important aspect of being a sustainability professional. Any skills and experiences that highlight how you are adaptable and able to communicate difficult subjects to diverse audiences would be beneficial in your resume or application. *Jeremy King— Campus Sustainability Coordinator, Denison University*[lxxx]

- When I hire someone, I am most concerned with their social competence in person. Most of the time I am looking for someone that is articulate and engaging above all else. That said I often need engineers or people who work behind the scenes whose resume and experience are vital to their success. For those individuals, I still need to be able to communicate with them and so I make sure every candidate has a communication style that works with my team even if they are not very outgoing. I ask a lot of questions about how they hear/listen and prefer to communicate. It's so important. *Claudia Capitini—Founder and Principal, Maven Consulting, LLC*[lxxxi]

- Excellent communication skills, both oral and written. *Jackie Drumheller— Sustainability Manager, Alaska Airlines*[lxxxii]

Strong People Skills

- Influencing others, collaborating with different people to achieve results, positive attitude, and persistence all important. *Jake Swenson—Director of Sustainability, Staples[lxxxiii]*

- In person, I look for someone who can authentically engage with me, wants to learn, is focused on continuous improvement, and has a passion for leading through empowerment rather than blame or judgment. *Brenna Davis—Director of Sustainability, Virginia Mason/Chair, WBCA[lxxxiv]*

Humility and Flexibility

- Also, is the person an 'all about me, me, me' type individual or are they a 'how can I help you, you, you' (Ex. coworkers, customers, community, etc.). Resourcefulness--if they get stuck creatively or technically, can they figure out a path out of the situation, who to talk to, how to get things restarted, etc. *Sean Schmidt—Office of Sustainability Assistant Director of Communications & Programs, University of Washington[lxxxv]*

Share Credit

- If you want to engage and energize the people you work with, you really need to give them credit for successes, you have to acknowledge the value in their ideas for change, and you have to own the failures – even if they aren't entirely yours to own. Some of the best sustainability professionals are the ones to who operate in the background. Never assume you are the smartest person in the room when it comes to sustainability. *Jeremy King— Campus Sustainability Coordinator, Denison University[lxxxvi]*

Ability to Build Relationships

- The ability to develop and maintain good relationships. In a company, the work of sustainability is never done in a vacuum. If you don't have good rapport with internal and external stakeholders, you will be very limited in your ability to get things done. It's not like accounting, where you can sit at a desk and "do accounting." Sustainability is all about influencing an organization to think differently; it's about collaborating to tackle big challenges. You can't do it alone. *Sarah Martinez—Sustainability Maven, Eco Products*[lxxxvii]

Both Quantitative and Qualitative

- Ability to be comfortable in both the quantitative and qualitative realms. Data and metrics are a huge part of sustainability, but so is the ability to tell your story, collaborate, and achieve buy-in. If you're too far on one end of the spectrum, you might struggle with mastering all aspects of the job. *Sarah Martinez—Sustainability Maven, Eco Products*[lxxxviii]

- Ability to discuss/display data in an interesting way. *Jackie Drumheller— Sustainability Manager, Alaska Airlines*[lxxxix]

Resume

- The two primarily things I look for in an application (resume/cover letter) are clear, concise writing and a demonstrated interest in the field (internships, volunteering, or other outside activities). *Maggie Schilling—Administrative Director, Northern Rockies Conservation Cooperative*[xc]

- I look to see if the person actually matches the required qualifications and skills, at a minimum addresses how their skill sets and experience make up for these requirements. Too often people apply for jobs where they want to work, but have not developed the skills to do the job. *Cynthia Figge—Co-Founder and COO, CSR Hub*[xci]

- Identify your strengths and transferable skills. You might not have the typical resume of other applicants, but that doesn't mean you aren't qualified to do a sustainability job. Many skills are transferable - communication, leadership, conflict resolution, creativity, the ability to think outside the box, and other skills will be important regardless of your career field and background. Identify your strengths and figure out how to communicate these in networking meetings, cover letters, and application materials. *Jo Opdyke Wilhelm—Senior Ecologist, King County Waste and Land Resources Division[xcii]*

Preparation

- During an interview, applicants must be prepared, punctual, and comfortable conversing about the position and the company. *Maggie Schilling—Administrative Director, Northern Rockies Conservation Cooperative[xciii]*

Initiative

- Initiative. My past hiring opportunities have been with summer interns. Given that, I simply do not interview (nor read the resume of) any student who has not made an effort to differentiate themselves by reaching out to me directly and personally. So many people just upload their resume and leave it at that. Since sustainability is generally about changing "the way we've always done things", I find that you need to be brave and show a lot of initiative to get things done. The way you approach your job search is my first clue whether you would be good at this or not. *Jackie Drumheller— Sustainability Manager, Alaska Airlines[xciv]*

- I look for someone who has ability (and desire) to work creatively while staying on task and timeline. That balance of idea flow, diligence and accountability is not always easy to find! *Molly Ray— Sr. Mgr Sustainability, Office Depot[xcv]*

- Ability and desire to actually deliver something. *Janice Lichtenwaldt—Sr. Mgr IT Communications, T-Mobile*[xcvi]

- Do they work hard? *Katie Mattis Sarver—CEO, Katie Mattis Consulting*[xcvii]

Know Yourself

- Personality and resourcefulness. Personality--does the person know who they are, what they are about, and what they want to do in life and does the person have a unique perspective on the world? *Sean Schmidt—Office of Sustainability Assistant Director of Communications & Programs, University of Washington*[xcviii]

Critical Thinking

- Demonstrated critical thinking and go-getter approach - ability to think critically and understand likely reactions of others to anticipate how to best position work, plan out approach to specific projects/problems, roll up sleeves and get things done. *Jake Swenson—Director of Sustainability, Staples*[xcix]

Curiosity

- Genuine curiosity and an interest in learning more. *Janice Lichtenwaldt—Sr. Mgr IT Communications, T-Mobile*[c]

- A natural curiosity to improve the status quo and a history of solving problems. *Matt O'Laughlin—Sustainability Manager, K2 Sports*[ci]

Team Players

- The intangibles. There are certain skills that can be learned and others that can't. I'm always looking for good communicators, natural leaders, and team players who demonstrate a collaborative spirit and an ability to work with a broad range of people. *Jo Opdyke Wilhelm—Senior Ecologist, King County Waste and Land Resources Division[cii]*

Balance

- Balance. I like to hire well rounded people - they need to have taken the classes and gained the experience and have done fairly well in school (this doesn't mean acing everything). But I also like to see that they have been active members of the community - playing sports, participating in music, dance, or theater, trying out internships, volunteering, traveling, or working a job while going through school, etc. This demonstrates the ability to multi-task, explore various interests, live passionately, and hopefully maintain a healthy work-life balance which is going to make someone a better worker. *Jo Opdyke Wilhelm—Senior Ecologist, King County Waste and Land Resources Group[ciii]*

Challenge Taker

- A tendency to put themselves in unfamiliar situations to learn and challenge their skills. *Matt O'Laughlin—Sustainability Manager, K2 Sports[civ]*

Positive Attitude

- A positive and enthusiastic perspective on life. The field of sustainability requires change agents, and these must be positive and enthusiastic to be effective. Doom and Gloom promotes fear with negative change. *Marianella Franklin—Chief Sustainability Officer, University of Texas Rio-Grande Valley[cv]*

- Patient Drive. Drive is a typical characteristic of candidates who seek to work in this field but it is critical to understand the need for both patience and persistence. *Marianella Franklin—Chief Sustainability Officer, University of Texas Rio-Grande Valley[cvi]*

Experience

- Real project experience or experience with organizations or people that have a reputation for innovation and action in sustainability. *Marsha Willard—CEO, Axis Performance Advisors[cvii]*

- I look for real world experience and an eclectic background. *Howard Sharfstein— Associate General Counsel – Environmental Sustainability, Kimberly Clark[cviii]*

Education/Credentials

- Credentials that I recognize – as in either a certificate or degree from a recognizable and credible institution. *Marsha Willard—CEO, Axis Performance Advisors[cix]*

Navigating Ambiguity

- Beyond demonstrated expertise in the sustainability field that suits the position, I would say 1) a true passion for the work and 2) the ability to navigate complexity and ambiguity. Working on sustainability issues is amazing, but it can also be very challenging. Career paths are not as linear as those in say accounting, and frankly some of the issues we work on (e.g. climate change) are sobering and long-term in nature. I want candidates that can thrive in this environment. *Michael Sadowski—Director, Innovation Scale & Partnerships, Nike, Inc[cx].*

If you had to tell a 30/40 something that is looking to do a career change, and wants to match their work with their values by getting into sustainability, what are the two most important things for them to know?

Prepare Financially

- Balance out making the change ASAP with knowing you might need to take a pay cut or get an unpaid internship. Having some money in savings to take the leap will mean you are much more flexible to take the right position that comes along. But don't wait. If you are unfulfilled in your current work, get out. You will lose your competitiveness and passion and will be stuck. *Dan Moore—CEO, Pandion Consulting and Facilitation[cxi]*

Take Care of Yourself

- Have self-care practices and prioritizing them at the same level as your work. Don't skip your yoga practice. Don't skip your kids' events. Do open mics. Make time for yourself. This is a way of life, not a job. *Derek Eisel—Director of Sales, Scope 5[cxii]*

Get Started Where You Are!

- Start with your current experience and find a job where you can still harness your current expertise while building your sustainability chops. For example, if you are a graphic designer, find a company that works on sustainable projects that is looking for someone with design experience. *Dan Moore—CEO Pandion Consulting and Facilitation[cxiii]*

- DON'T do a career change. Figure out how to bring sustainability to where you currently work. Good ideas that have a strong business case can innovate and revitalize the place you currently work. If you're thinking is on and you present a good pitch for how matching your values to the company will ultimately help the company improve and expand its business, leadership should get it and be excited for you to stay and implement your ideas. *Sean Schmidt— Office of Sustainability Assistant Director of Communications & Programs, University of Washington*[cxiv]

- I would advise the person to seek out the CSR department in their current company, and do volunteer work with that group. Learn how the function works in your current company and find ways to build your skill set while doing your current job. Many people move into sustainability roles laterally inside a company they already understand. *Cynthia Figge—Co-Founder and COO, CSR Hub*[cxv]

- Start by assessing whether you can bring your values and interest in sustainability into your current role or company. A growing number of companies (including mine) are integrating sustainability into core business functions like marketing and design, and there may be opportunities in such functions. *Michael Sadowski—Director, Innovation Scale & Partnerships, Nike, Inc.* [cxvi]

Due Diligence

- Because sustainability is still relatively new for most organizations and businesses, you have a tremendous opportunity to use that to craft how that organization or business will approach sustainability. *Jeremy King— Campus Sustainability Coordinator, Denison University*[cxvii]

Education/ Credentials

- I would advise the person to go back to school, at least a certificate. S/he will be competing with people who have focused their education on integrating sustainability and so if the 30/40 something has no sustainability education and no sustainability experience; it will be tough to break into this area. *Cynthia Figge— Co-Founder and COO, CSR Hub*[cxviii]

Leverage Past Experience

- Leverage your existing knowledge and core competencies. I find that most successful sustainability professionals tend to be entrepreneurial in their endeavors. The prior work experienced has value. It takes a unique person to cognitively make linkages and communicate the value proposition offered in employing sustainability practices among the traditional, non-sustainability community. *Patrick Drum— Portfolio Manager & Research Analyst, Saturna Capital[cxix]*

- Being successful in a sustainability-related career takes the same skill set as nearly any other career. When making a career change and searching for jobs, play that aspect up. Highlight some of the challenges you faced in your previous career/job and how you had to adapt and overcome. Your ability to do so makes you a better candidate. That is the name of the game in Sustainability. *Jeremy King— Campus Sustainability Coordinator, Denison University[cxx]*

- Expertise in finance, HR, marketing, administration, and/or fundraising would be of great value to most organizations. *Maggie Schilling—Administrative Director, Northern Rockies Conservation Cooperative[cxxi]*

- Make a slow turn rather than reaching for a dramatic change in direction. Find ways to build on existing skills and experience by connecting them to sustainability in a way you can sensibly explain. *Jon Kroman—CEO, Kroman Law[cxxii]*

- Your previous work and life experience brings value and a new perspective to an industry that continues to evolve. Don't be afraid to share those insights even though you aren't an "industry expert." *Katie Mattis Sarver—CEO, Katie Mattis Consulting[cxxiii]*

- Analyze your past experience to extract your strongest skills and how these can be redirected into your new/hidden passion. Be confident in sharing your past experience and how it ties to the corporation, institutional, employer, or client interest and most importantly what you can offer to build their SUCCESS! *Marianella Franklin—Chief Sustainability Officer, University of Texas Rio-Grande Valley*[cxxiv]

Potentially Stepping Down a Notch

- Don't be bummed out if you have to take a more junior position. A lot of people think if they care about sustainability, then they can be a sustainability manager. Honestly, I find that a little insulting! There is *some* skill needed to do what I do. A mid-career transition can mean going down a rung or two on the corporate ladder, but if this is a career path you really want to explore, it will be worth it. *Sarah Martinez—Sustainability Maven, Eco Products*[cxxv]

- I think many mid-career professionals looking to make a switch to the field are surprised how competitive it is, given the generally lower wages. Be prepared to start a bit closer to the bottom than you might hope. *Maggie Schilling—Administrative Director, Northern Rockies Conservation Cooperative*[cxxvi]

Play A Supporting Role

- If you are willing to play a support role to the people "doing the work" of the nonprofit--i.e. the program directors--you will have a much greater chance of breaking in to the field. *Maggie Schilling— Administrative Director, Northern Rockies Conservation Cooperative*[cxxvii]

Perseverance

- Just like the new graduates - you may need patience, persistence, and commitment to make the career shift work. It might not be easy or come immediately. *Jo Opdyke Wilhelm—Senior Ecologist, King County Waste and Land Resources Division[cxxviii]*

Get Help

- Get help. Not *that* kind of help, but hire a career coach, life coach, friend, recruiter, or similar person to help you. There is nothing better than outside help in repositioning your resume, thinking about your goals differently, getting another set or two of eyes on everything you are doing, or reminding you that you are not, in fact, crazy. You might have to completely restructure your resume and update your wardrobe - that often seems ludicrous if you are used to one industry or a particular way of presenting yourself - but stay open, and go for it. *Claudia Capitini—Founder and Principal, Maven Consulting, LLC[cxxix]*

Competition is Fierce

- You're up against a lot of competition. *Jackie Drumheller— Sustainability Manager, Alaska Airlines[cxxx]*

Apply CSR in Traditional Business

- You don't have to be in a sustainability specific role to make a huge impact. At the end of the day, most of the biggest impact areas are "owned" by traditional functional departments. A product design head or senior executive at a consumer goods manufacturer can do more to advance sustainability in a year than a chief sustainability officer by deciding to integrate sustainability into design process holistically. *Jake Swenson—Director of Sustainability, Staples[cxxxi]*

- If you are considering corporate sustainability functions, consider how your experience and skill set translate. These corporate functions will benefit from your time in the "business" (finance, marketing, etc.). *Michael Sadowski—Director, Innovation Scale & Partnerships, Nike, Inc[cxxxii]*

Reality Check—This Stuff Is Hard!

- Learning sustainability isn't hard, but change is hard, and sustainability is really about change. You can pick up sustainability by reading a collection of really good books, taking a week or month long course, and networking with sustainability experts. However, corporate sustainability is about understanding current business and changing how business gets done more than anything else. Change can be hard, especially in areas outside of traditional cost saving areas of sustainability like energy and waste. Supply chain sustainability is hard. Design for the circular economy is hard. Especially for established companies who were not built to integrate sustainability. If you are used to measuring success by results you are able to drive on a monthly or annual basis then you could be very frustrated by the time it can take to advance your goals in a sustainability role. Really important for you to know what you are getting into depending on the company and role you are looking at. *Jake Swenson—Director of Sustainability, Staples[cxxxiii]*

Go For It!

- This was me. I made a career change in my 30's and it enriched my life to get off of the track I was on and go for something more in line with my values. So first I'd say, go for it! *Molly Ray—Sr. Mgr Sustainability, Office Depot[cxxxiv]*

- It won't happen overnight. Most of us in our 30's and 40's that made this type of change had to slowly implement this plan through: education (whilst working a full time job in some cases), balancing family commitments (that we maybe didn't have the last time around) and the diligence to stick through the 'starting over' process. However, I'm a firm believer that working towards your goal(s), however slowly or incrementally, is where a sense of purpose and true personal fulfillment lives. *Molly Ray—Sr. Mgr Sustainability, Office Depot[cxxxv]*

- Sustainability is in the eye of the beholder and a lens through which you see the world. Reframe your experience into terms used by sustainability professionals. *Howard Sharfstein— Associate General Counsel – Environmental Sustainability, Kimberly Clark[cxxxvi]*

Age Isn't Important

- I don't think age is a factor. Skills and enthusiasm (demonstrated by the candidates work experience and outside activities) are most important. *Eli Reich—Chief Alchemist, Alchemy Goods[cxxxvii]*

Tailor Your Expertise

- Know your stuff and be specific. Sustainability is a wide field. You could focus on social justice, renewable energy, organic products, carbon emissions . . . and the list goes on. Find the area that most speaks to you and become an expert. *Janice Lichtenwaldt—Sr. Mgr IT Communications[cxxxviii]*

Volunteer

- There are many others doing the same thing. Find the fastest way to get involved, get experience and make an impact. This may not be through traditional education or career path routes. *Matt O'Laughlin—Sustainability Manager, K2 Sports[cxxxix]*

Connect With Your Passion

- Sustainability is a broad subject matter...Review the UN Global Goals for Sustainable Development and pick the one that resonates with your PASSION. Redirecting your career will only succeed if you have faith in your passion. Your greatest strength is in your passion! Once you have selected a goal conduct a quick SWOT analysis of the region/company/institution you plan to target to research and strengthen your knowledge and find your areas of opportunity. *Marianella Franklin—Chief Sustainability Officer, University of Texas Rio-Grande Valley[cxl]*

Respect Other's Opinions

- Living your passion is good for you, but will still require that you work with, honor and respect, and effectively manage others who may not share your world view. *Marsha Willard—Co-Founder, International Society of Sustainability Professionals, ISSP[cxli]*

Language

- The notion that they don't get it doesn't suffice but rather offers an important hint that a clearer and more simplified message is needed. *Patrick Drum— Portfolio Manager & Research Analyst, Saturna Capital[cxlii]*

Know Yourself

- Know and understand what is truly driving your career change. Be specific with yourself about how you want to approach "starting over" (which isn't really starting over, but applying your talents to a field that has more meaning). *Katie Mattis Sarver—CEO, Katie Mattis Consulting[cxliii]*

Create Your Own Job

- You can always do what I did when I was 40-something -- create a sustainability position for yourself at your current place of employment. Your first step would be to start or join a green team and identify some projects that will save the company money. After a few years of relentlessly proving the case that sustainability is valuable to your organization, you just might have created a job for yourself. There are many good resources in books and on the web to help you get started. *Jackie Drumheller— Sustainability Manager, Alaska Airlines*[cxliv]

What is something that an aspiring sustainability professional should know, that nobody will tell them?

<u>Language</u>

- If you use statistics and convincing language, saying something is sustainable will make it so. *Howard Sharfstein— Associate General Counsel – Environmental Sustainability, Kimberly Clark[cxlv]*

<u>Financial Preparation</u>

- It's really hard to find sustainability work and you'll likely make more money with your intelligence and organizational savvy doing something else (at least in the first many years). Go into it knowing and embracing the challenges over a long term (think decades). *Derek Eisel—Director of Sales, Scope 5[cxlvi]*

<u>Keep Current Skills</u>

- Sustainable business skills are changing every profession. It's now not its own profession, like knowing how to use a computer. *Kevin Hagen—CSR Director, Iron Mountain[cxlvii]*

<u>It Goes Beyond Your Job</u>

- Don't expect to exclusively change the world with your day job. You also need to be working in your community on meaningful projects and initiatives. Sustainability is a movement, and that mission needs to never be overshadowed by your need to make a living. *Dan Moore—CEO, Pandion Consulting[cxlviii]*

Passion Problem

- Your passion may be seen as a liability. More conservative, conventional managers may believe your enthusiasm and perspective make you blind to the realities of business or legitimate solutions. Ensure you establish your credibility in combination with expressing your passion. *Janice Lichtenwaldt—Sr. Mgr IT Communications, T-Mobile[cxlix]*

Respect Other's Opinions

- If you rest on your environmental values to get a job – you'll be disappointed. So much of being a successful sustainability professional is about building relationships and building consensus, not projecting your values on to others. *Jeremy King— Campus Sustainability Coordinator, Denison University[cl]*

Reality Check

- This can be a lonely job. Few companies have teams of sustainability managers. You are often a lone wolf. *Sarah Martinez—Sustainability Maven, Eco Products[cli]*

- It's a psychological roller coaster every single day at work. When you achieve a success … it's a real high… but then there are many days where you are beating your head against the wall over and over while nothing changes and no one listens. *Jackie Drumheller— Sustainability Manager, Alaska Airlines[clii]*

- Sustainability is a popular buzz word, but the real work is challenging. Ensure you're in it for the right reasons and up for the battle. *Matt O'Laughlin—Sustainability Manager, K2 Sports[cliii]*

Change Management is Hard!

- If there is not a clear direction from the top that sustainability is important, it can be an uphill battle to get internal staff engaged. Think about it – you are adding to people's plates and/or trying to get them to change the way they do their job. And really… who are you to tell them this?! Be aware that often the role is one of change management and influencing without authority. Hence, the importance of developing good relationships and achieving buy-in. *Sarah Martinez—Sustainability Maven, Eco Products*[cliv]

- Don't underestimate the incredible power of culture, behavior, and perceptions when it comes to rejecting or embracing sustainability. There is still a huge need for, and power in, connecting emotionally with customers and employees to drive behavior you want to see. When I was in school, I thought it was all about making the business case. Making a business case is obviously important and it always helps if customers ask for sustainability, but the longer I've been in this space the more I realize the power of culture, behavior, and perceptions.
  If you understand human behavior and use effective techniques to try and drive behavior/perception change, I believe sustainability practitioners can be much more successful in their roles. A lot more brands are focusing on telling stories and humanizing sustainability to connect their brands to purpose and it can be very powerful if done well. *Jake Swenson—Director of Sustainability, Staples*[clv]

- There are many successful models for institutionalizing sustainability regardless of private, public, educational, or corporate sector. It is very important to spend time in understanding political and economic structures before planning any kind of strategic plan. This is the foundation. It will save time and money from guaranteed roadblocks if done in advance regardless of proposed model. Some models are top down while other are bottom up.
  I highly recommend taking the time to work from both ends, ensuring all stakeholders later meet on common ground. Master plan your strategy! Some initiatives take longer than others. Do not make

the mistake of going for all the low hanging fruit. Review carefully and alternate your projects (low and high hanging fruit) in phases for the best return on investment. *Marianella Franklin—Chief Sustainability Officer, University of Texas Rio-Grande Valley[clvi]*

- It would seem based on data points such as the number of companies reporting on their sustainability efforts that most companies "get" sustainability. A 2010 Accenture and UN Global Compact survey of CEOs globally found that 93% believed that sustainability was important to their company's future success and 81% said that their companies had already embedded sustainability. I think it's fair to say that these survey responses do not represent the current state of corporate sustainability.
  True integration remains a work in progress at most companies. Senior management may voice their support for the work, but the real work happens in trying to embed sustainability into the middle layers of companies – the teams that make product, manage logistics, etc. The sustainability professional needs to come equipped to educate, inspire, cajole, convince – and do so for functions with different motivations. *Michael Sadowski—Director, Innovation Scale & Partnerships, Nike, Inc. [clvii]*

How Others May Perceive You

- If you can build the life you want and find work that is meaningful and fulfilling in sustainability, you will be surprised at how awesome everyone thinks your job is (even if it's not that awesome all the time). I think deep down, most people want to work in ways that better others or the planet. Unfortunately, not everyone has that opportunity. Aside from the obvious benefit of eliminating job-envy on your part, it is really great to see inspiration in others. The world needs a lot of help - uplifting someone simply because your work aligns with your passion in a cool field like sustainability is one of the most subtle-yet-fabulous things we have going for us in this field. *Claudia Capitini—Founder and Principal, Maven Consulting, LLC[clviii]*

Career/Life Planning

- If "climbing the ladder" is very important to you, think hard about whether or not to start a family, as these two things do not always seem to be very compatible. *Maggie Schilling—Administrative Director, Northern Rockies Conservation Cooperative*[clix]

Networking—Look for Casual Ways to Make Things Happen

- Learn how to play golf. Or learn how to make a lot of different cocktails. Almost all conversations that actually lead to change happen on the golf course or over drinks. If you go the route of presenting something at work, it tends to be all formal and has to go through cost/benefit analysis and a lot of people that will oppose things just for the sake of opposing them. But if you happen to run into the CEO on golf course or over drinks and strike up a casual conversation (and your elevator speech better be spot on), you're likely to get things to happen. *Sean Schmidt—Office of Sustainability Assistant Director of Communications & Programs, University of Washington*[clix]

Perseverance

- That there will be those that don't believe in your vision, mission or path. Well, maybe we hear this but it is always a little disconcerting to encounter. The world is changing quickly and while more and more people are unable to deny science and our connectedness as humans on this planet, there is a contingent that has not and will not necessarily change in their lifetime. You can accept and move around that as there has never been a profession where you don't have roadblocks and potential naysayers. In the case of sustainability, there is so much good and meaningful work to be done and it's important to stay aligned with your purpose and path. *Molly Ray— Sr. Mgr Sustainability, Office Depot*[clxi]

<u>Business Case</u>

- If you can't make a sound business case for a sustainable initiative or business, it will fall on deaf ears. *Eli Reich—Chief Alchemist, Alchemy Goods[clxii]*

- To me, corporate sustainability is not a cause or movement; it is an essential principle of a sound business plan. It's not a feel-good platform, but an area of focus that drives efficiency and revenue just as other areas of the business do so. *Katie Mattis Sarver—CEO, Katie Mattis Consulting[clxiii]*

<u>It Requires Being Entrepreneurial at Times</u>

- "We've all been making this up as we go along and to a large extent that is still true. Honor the work that has come before but be creative and experimental. Be prepared to build the bike as you are riding it. *Marsha Willard—Co-Founder, International Society of Sustainability Professionals, ISSP[clxiv]*

- The field of sustainability is nascent, despite over 25 years of development within many companies. It requires a great deal of entrepreneurial spirit, perseverance and creativity. This is a field for inventors and collaborators and people who "see ahead." If this fits your personality and passion, go for it. *Cynthia Figge—Co-Founder and COO, CSR Hub[clxv]*

- This is a bit scary because there's no clearly defined path. But it's also exciting and a chance to be entrepreneurial. Be ready for both aspects. *Dan Stonington—Executive Director, NW National Resource Group[clxvi]*

CSR in Traditional Business

- Be realistic and specific in defining "sustainability professional" for yourself. All kinds of disciplines- marketing, finance, law, HR, government relations- can have sustainability elements and may fit your interests, skills and experience better than the high profile corporate CSR and consulting professionals you may associate with the term. Pick your path. If you're too vague about wanting to be a "sustainability professional", you'll have no credibility and consequently no basis for expecting success. *Jon Kroman—CEO, Kroman Law*[clxvii]

Nobody Knows It All

- Nobody knows it all. There are experts out there, who know a lot, but no one knows it all and no one has all the answers for how to green the world. You, and others, likely have some valuable insights to contribute. Be confident in your ideas - no matter how wacky they might initially seem. *Jo Opdyke Wilhelm—Senior Ecologist, King County Waste and Land Resources Division*[clxviii]

Assess Your Organization

- Try to find out as soon as possible whether the organization/business you work for wants to appear to be sustainable or whether they really want to make systemic changes to improve the bottom line or increase marketability. There is a huge difference and if you are prepared to work in one environment and find yourself in the other, you will be disappointed daily. *Jeremy King— Campus Sustainability Coordinator, Denison University*[clxix]

Take Care of Yourself

- Sustainability work is really change management, which can get stressful. As a change agent, you need to have excellent self-care to keep from getting burned out and to stay healthy. Self care means taking care of your mind, body, and spirit. Exercise, eat right, meditate, get acupuncture, see a therapist -- do whatever it takes to feel whole, healthy and happy. You need to be resilient to stay in this work for a few decades like I have. *Brenna Davis—Director of Sustainability, Virginia Mason/ Chair, WBCA[clxx]*

Change Management is Necessary

- To be a successful sustainability professional you have to be a strategic thinker and understand the difference between strategy and tactics. A tactical thinker will make a series of decisions to solve individual problems, whereas the strategist will evaluate the system as a whole – all the problems – to plan out a cohesive course of action. If you find yourself saying "pick your battles" you are already beginning to understand the difference. *Jeremy King— Campus Sustainability Coordinator, Denison University[clxxi]*

  Everyone has a hidden agenda – understand that and work to uncover it. *Jeremy King—Sustainability Director, Denison University[clxxii]*

<u>Put It in a Language They Can Understand</u>

- As I often tell people, sustainability is a lot like teaching high school math/science – every day you are faced with an audience that doesn't understand what you are saying, doesn't generally care why you are saying it, and certainly doesn't see how this relates to their lives. It is your job to find ways to connect and make it meaningful – or at least give them a sense of purpose. *Jeremy King— Campus Sustainability Coordinator, Denison University*[clxxiii]

- There are always many ways to reach a goal. Here's a scenario: A Sustainability Director has been charged with reducing her company's carbon footprint. She holds meeting after meeting about why this is important, but gets very little traction. The CFO only cares about the bottom line and thinks efforts to reduce the carbon footprint will cost more money. The Facilities Director thinks climate change and carbon footprints are a hoax.
There is very little common ground in this scenario. To solve the problem, the Sustainability Director drops the rhetoric of carbon footprints and climate change and instead talks about energy-efficiency, return on investment, and cost avoidance. Now the CFO is listening and the Facilities Director is pleased that more emphasis will be placed on running the physical plant more efficiently and effectively. In the end, reduced energy use leads to reduce carbon footprints. *Jeremy King— Campus Sustainability Coordinator, Denison University*[clxxiv]

CONCLUSION AND PUTTING IT ALL TOGETHER

In conclusion, I know that looking for a job, adding sustainability to your current role, or embarking on a career change can be nerve racking, difficult, and an emotional roller-coaster, but you can do it!

The information, tips and worksheets included in this book are designed to help you through the process. You are not alone. Every single person that goes through a job search or career change has ups and downs. You'll face moments of excitement, as well as disappointments and moments of self-doubt, but hang in there. The most important aspect of trying to get a job in sustainability is perseverance.

You can do this. Get started. Get clear as to who you are and what you want to do. Target and tailor your job search. Network, execute, and remember to prep for every interview, even if it's just an informational interview. And incorporate the tips from the Masters, and you'll be well on your way to landing your dream green job.

Good luck. We are at a point in time when we need everyone possible joining us in the fight. We face unprecedented social, political, and environmental challenges. So don't delay. Find your sustainability job today!

ENDNOTES

[i] Jake Swenson—Director of Sustainability, Staples

[ii] Dan Stonington—Executive Director, NW Natural Resource Group

[iii] Cynthia Figge—Co-Founder and COO, CSR Hub

[iv] Jo Opdyke Wilhelm—Senior Ecologist, King County Water and Land Resources Division

[v] Jackie Drumheller— Sustainability Manager, Alaska Airlines

[vi] Brenna Davis—Director of Sustainability, Virginia Mason/ Chair, WBCA

[vii] Sean Schmidt—Office of Sustainability Assistant Director of Communications & Programs, University of Washington

[viii] Matt O'Laughlin— Sustainability Manager, K2 Sports

[ix] Marianella Franklin—Chief Sustainability Officer, University of Texas Rio-Grande Valley

[x] Sarah Martinez—Sustainability Maven, Eco Products

[xi] Janice Lichtenwaldt—Sr. Mgr IT Communications, T-Mobile

[xii] Kevin Hagen—CSR Director, Iron Mountain

[xiii] Derek Eisel—Director of Sales, Scope 5

[xiv] Cynthia Figge—Co-Founder and COO, CSR Hub

[xv] Patrick Drum— Portfolio Manager & Research Analyst, Saturna Capital

[xvi] Jeremy King— Campus Sustainability Coordinator, Denison University

[xvii] Brenna Davis—Director of Sustainability, Virginia Mason/ Chair, WBCA

[xviii] Jo Opdyke Wilhelm—Senior Ecologist, King County Waste and Land Resources Division

[xix] Claudia Capitini—Founder and Principal, Maven Consulting, LLC

[xx] Jon Kroman—CEO, Kroman Law

[xxi] Jon Kroman—CEO, Kroman Law

[xxii] Claudia Capitini—Founder and Principal, Maven Consulting, LLC

[xxiii] Jobvite. 2015 Recruiter Nation Survey. http://www.jobvite.com/wp-content/uploads/2015/09/jobvite_recruiter_nation_2015.pdf

[xxiv] Claudia Capitini—Founder and Principal, Maven Consulting, LLC

[xxv] Sean Schmidt—Office of Sustainability Assistant Director of Communications & Programs, University of Washington

[xxvi] Jo Opdyke Wilhelm—Senior Ecologist, King County Waste and Land Resources Division)

[xxvii] Dan Stonington—Executive Director, NW Natural Resource Group

[xxviii] Sarah Martinez—Sustainability Maven, Eco Product

[xxix] Jeremy King— Campus Sustainability Coordinator, Denison University

[xxx] Derek Eisel—Director of Sales, Scope 5

[xxxi] Jackie Drumheller— Sustainability Manager, Alaska Airlines

[xxxii] Kevin Hagen, —CSR Director, Iron Mountain

[xxxiii] Dan Moore—CEO, Pandion Consulting and Facilitation

[xxxiv] Dan Moore—CEO, Pandion Consulting and Facilitation

[xxxv] Sarah Martinez—Sustainability Maven, Eco Products

[xxxvi] Maggie Schilling—Executive Director, Teton Science School

[xxxvii] Jake Swenson—Director of Sustainability, Staples

[xxxviii] Cynthia Figge—Co-Founder and COO, CSR Hub

[xxxix] Dan Moore—CEO, Pandion Consulting and Facilitation

[xl] Claudia Capitini—Founder and Principal, Maven Consulting, LLC

[xli] Patrick Drum— Portfolio Manager & Research Analyst, Saturna Capital

[xlii] Sarah Martinez—Sustainability Maven, Eco Products

[xliii] Claudia Capitini—Founder and Principal, Maven Consulting, LLC

[xliv] Eli Reich—Chief Alchemist, Alchemy Goods

[xlv] Janice Lichtenwaldt—Sr. Mgr IT Communications, T-Mobile

[xlvi] Jeremy King— Campus Sustainability Coordinator, Denison University

[xlvii] Jon Kroman—CEO, Kroman Law
[xlviii] Jeremy King— Campus Sustainability Coordinator, Denison University
[xlix] Molly Ray—Sr. Mgr Sustainability, Office Depot
[l] Sarah Martinez—Sustainability Maven, Eco Products
[li] Maggie Schilling—Executive Director, Teton Science School
[lii] Marsha Willard—CEO, Axis Performance Advisors
[liii] Maggie Schilling—Executive Director, Teton Science School
[liv] Jo Opdyke Wilhelm—Senior Ecologist, King County Waste and Land Resources Division
[lv] Marianella Franklin— Chief Sustainability Officer, University of Texas-Rio Grande Valley
[lvi] Brenna Davis—Director of Sustainability, Virginia Mason/ Chair, WBCA
[lvii] Claudia Capitini—Founder and Principal, Maven Consulting, LLC
[lviii] Matt O'Laughlin—Sustainability Manager, K2 Sports
[lix] Marsha Willard—CEO, Axis Performance Advisors
[lx] Michael Sadowski—Director, Innovation Scale & Partnerships, Nike, Inc.
[lxi] Sean Schmidt—Office of Sustainability Assistant Director of Communications & Programs, University of Washington
[lxii] Jake Swenson—Director of Sustainability, Staples
[lxiii] Jake Swenson—Director of Sustainability, Staples
[lxiv] Jake Swenson—Director of Sustainability, Staples
[lxv] Howard Sharfstein— Associate General Counsel – Environmental Sustainability, Kimberly Clark
[lxvi] Michael Sadowski—Director, Innovation Scale & Partnerships, Nike, Inc
[lxvii] Molly Ray—Sr. Mgr Sustainability, Office Depot
[lxviii] Michael Sadowski—Director, Innovation Scale & Partnerships, Nike, Inc
[lxix] Janice Lichtenwaldt—Sr. Mgr IT Communications, T-Mobile
[lxx] Matt O'Laughlin—Sustainability Manager, K2 Sports
[lxxi] Cynthia Figge—Co-Founder and COO, CSR Hub
[lxxii] Marianella Franklin—Chief Sustainability Officer, University of Texas Rio-Grande Valley
[lxxiii] Marsha Willard—CEO, Axis Performance Advisors
[lxxiv] Jon Kroman—CEO, Kroman Law
[lxxv] Derek Eisel—Director of Sales, Scope 5
[lxxvi] Eli Reich—Chief Alchemist, Alchemy Goods
[lxxvii] Dan Stonington—Executive Director, NW Natural Resource Group
[lxxviii] Dan Moore—CEO, Pandion Consulting and Facilitation
[lxxix] Patrick Drum—Portfolio Manager & Research Analyst, Saturna Capital
[lxxx] Jeremy King— Campus Sustainability Coordinator, Denison University
[lxxxi] Claudia Capitini—Founder and Principal, Maven Consulting, LLC
[lxxxii] Jackie Drumheller— Sustainability Manager, Alaska Airlines
[lxxxiii] Jake Swenson—Director of Sustainability, Staples
[lxxxiv] Brenna Davis—Director of Sustainability, Virginia Mason/Chair, WBCA
[lxxxv] Sean Schmidt—Office of Sustainability Assistant Director of Communications & Programs, University of Washington
[lxxxvi] Jeremy King— Campus Sustainability Coordinator, Denison University
[lxxxvii] Sarah Martinez—Sustainability Maven, Eco Products
[lxxxviii] Sarah Martinez—Sustainability Maven, Eco Products
[lxxxix] Jackie Drumheller— Sustainability Manager, Alaska Airlines
[xc] Maggie Schilling—Executive Director, Teton Science School
[xci] Cynthia Figge—Co-Founder and COO, CSR Hub
[xcii] Jo Opdyke Wilhelm—Senior Ecologist, King County Waste and Land Resources Division
[xciii] Maggie Schilling—Executive Director, Teton Science School
[xciv] Jackie Drumheller— Sustainability Manager, Alaska Airlines
[xcv] Molly Ray—Sr. Mgr Sustainability, Office Depot

xcvi Janice Lichtenwaldt—Sr. Mgr IT Communications, T-Mobile
xcvii Katie Mattis Sarver—CEO, Business Development and Event Consultant
xcviii Sean Schmidt—Office of Sustainability Assistant Director of Communications & Programs, University of Washington
xcix Jake Swenson—Director of Sustainability, Staples
c Janice Lichtenwaldt—Sr. Mgr IT Communications, T-Mobile
ci Matt O'Laughlin—Sustainability Manager, K2 Sports
cii Jo Opdyke Wilhelm—Senior Ecologist, King County Waste and Land Resources Division
ciii Jo Opdyke Wilhelm—Senior Ecologist, King County Waste and Land Resources Division
civ Matt O'Laughlin—Sustainability Manager, K2 Sports
cv Marianella Franklin—Chief Sustainability Officer, University of Texas Rio-Grande Valley
cvi Marianella Franklin—Chief Sustainability Officer, University of Texas Rio-Grande Valley
cvii Marsha Willard—CEO, Axis Performance Advisors
cviii Howard Sharfstein— Associate General Counsel – Environmental Sustainability, Kimberly Clark
cix Marsha Willard—CEO, Axis Performance Advisors
cx Michael Sadowski—Director, Innovation Scale & Partnerships, Nike, Inc
cxi Dan Moore—CEO, Pandion Consulting and Facilitation
cxii Derek Eisel—Director of Sales, Scope 5
cxiii Dan Moore—CEO Pandion Consulting and Facilitation
cxiv Sean Schmidt—Office of Sustainability Assistant Director of Communications & Programs, University of Washington
cxv Cynthia Figge—Co-Founder and COO, CSR Hub
cxvi Michael Sadowski—Director, Innovation Scale & Partnerships, Nike, Inc
cxvii Jeremy King— Campus Sustainability Coordinator, Denison University
cxviii Cynthia Figge—Co-Founder and COO, CSR Hub
cxix Patrick Drum— Portfolio Manager & Research Analyst, Saturna Capital
cxx Jeremy King— Campus Sustainability Coordinator, Denison University
cxxi Maggie Schilling—Executive Director, Teton Science School
cxxii Jon Kroman—CEO, Kroman Law
cxxiii Katie Mattis Sarver—CEO, Business Development and Event Consultant
cxxiv Marianella Franklin—Chief Sustainability Officer, University of Texas Rio-Grande Valley
cxxv Sarah Martinez—Sustainability Maven, Eco Products
cxxvi Maggie Schilling—Executive Director, Teton Science School
cxxvii Maggie Schilling—Executive Director, Teton Science School
cxxviii Jo Opdyke Wilhelm—Senior Ecologist, King County Waste and Land Resources Division
cxxix Claudia Capitini—Founder and Principal, Maven Consulting, LLC
cxxx Jackie Drumheller— Sustainability Manager, Alaska Airlines
cxxxi Jake Swenson—Director of Sustainability, Staples
cxxxii Michael Sadowski—Director, Innovation Scale & Partnerships, Nike, Inc
cxxxiii Jake Swenson—Director of Sustainability, Staples
cxxxiv Molly Ray—Sr. Mgr Sustainability, Office Depot
cxxxv Molly Ray—Sr. Mgr Sustainability, Office Depot
cxxxvi Howard Sharfstein— Associate General Counsel – Environmental Sustainability, Kimberly Clark
cxxxvii Eli Reich—Chief Alchemist, Alchemy Goods
cxxxviii Janice Lichtenwaldt—Sr. Mgr IT Communications
cxxxix Matt O'Laughlin—Sustainability Manager, K2 Sports
cxl Marianella Franklin—Chief Sustainability Officer, University of Texas Rio-Grande Valley
cxli Marsha Willard—CEO, Axis Performance Advisors
cxlii Patrick Drum— Portfolio Manager & Research Analyst, Saturna Capital
cxliii Katie Mattis Sarver—CEO, Business Development and Event Consultant

[cxliv] Jackie Drumheller— Sustainability Manager, Alaska Airlines
[cxlv] Howard Sharfstein— Associate General Counsel – Environmental Sustainability, Kimberly Clark
[cxlvi] Derek Eisel—Director of Sales, Scope 5
[cxlvii] Kevin Hagen—CSR Director, Iron Mountain
[cxlviii] Dan Moore—CEO, Pandion Consulting
[cxlix] Janice Lichtenwaldt—Sr. Mgr IT Communications, T-Mobile
[cl] Jeremy King— Campus Sustainability Coordinator, Denison University
[cli] Sarah Martinez—Sustainability Maven, Eco Products
[clii] Jackie Drumheller—Sustainability Manager, Alaska Airlines
[cliii] Matt O'Laughlin—Sustainability Manager, K2 Sports
[cliv] Sarah Martinez—Sustainability Maven, Eco Products
[clv] Jake Swenson—Director of Sustainability, Staples
[clvi] Marianella Franklin—Chief Sustainability Officer, University of Texas Rio-Grande Valley

[clviii] Claudia Capitini—Founder and Principal, Maven Consulting, LLC
[clix] Maggie Schilling—Executive Director, Teton Science School
[clx] Sean Schmidt—Office of Sustainability Assistant Director of Communications & Programs, University of Washington
[clxi] Molly Ray—Sr. Mgr Sustainability, Office Depot
[clxii] Eli Reich—Chief Alchemist, Alchemy Goods
[clxiii] Katie Mattis Sarver—CEO, Business Development and Event Consultant
[clxiv] Marsha Willard—CEO, Axis Performance Advisors
[clxv] Cynthia Figge—Co-Founder and COO, CSR Hub
[clxvi] Dan Stonington—Executive Director, NW National Resource Group
[clxvii] Jon Kroman—CEO, Kroman Law
[clxviii] Jo Opdyke Wilhelm—Senior Ecologist, King County Waste and Land Resources Division
[clxix] Jeremy King— Campus Sustainability Coordinator, Denison University
[clxx] Brenna Davis—Director of Sustainability, Virginia Mason/ Chair, WBCA
[clxxi] Jeremy King— Campus Sustainability Coordinator, Denison University
[clxxii] Jeremy King—Campus Sustainability Coordinator, Denison University
[clxxii] Michael Sadowski—Director, Innovation Scale & Partnerships, Nike, Inc
[clxxiii] Jeremy King— Campus Sustainability Coordinator, Denison University
[clxxiv] Jeremy King— Campus Sustainability Coordinator, Denison University